THE

DEAD

ANIMAL

HANDBOOK

HELL PRESS
UNIVERSITY OF HELL PRESS

THE DEAD ANIMAL HANDBOOK

an anthology of contemporary poetry

Edited by CAM AWKWARD-RICH & SAM SAX

HELL PRESS
UNIVERSITY OF HELL PRESS

This book published by University of Hell Press.
WWW.UNIVERSITYOFHELLPRESS.COM

© 2017 University of Hell Press

Book Design & Layout by Jeremy John Parker
WWW.JEREMYJOHNPARKER.COM/DESIGN

Published in the United States of America.
ISBN 978-1-938753-23-7

# INTRODUCTION

The Dead Animal Handbook began in the basement of an illegal arts venue in the Bay Area's Mission District. Alongside contributor Nic Alea, we were running a poetry open mic whose only goal was to not be awful and for the most part we succeeded. The audience was largely drunks and punks and hipsters and queers and weirdos and queirdos and as the weeks stumbled into years we noticed a theme emerging from that revolving eclectic glee club of writers. The figure of the dead animal reared its zombie head across countless poems: the sorrow dog, the exploited farm mule, the struck deer, the diseased mosquito, the waterfowl shot through the heart, and more. Most often we saw the dead animal used as a lens to plumb what it is to be this bizarre human animal on this strangely hospitable planet sprinting through darkness.

Curious, we threw together a quick collection for our two-year anniversary, composed of the folks who religiously attended the show.

As we reached out to writers we admired to solicit work, one after the other responded, perhaps a bit aghast, *How did you know that's my thing?* As it turns out, the history of writing is the history of animal death. The earliest examples of human creativity in written signs – cave paintings – often depict animals and while we have a good sense of when these forms of image-based communication originated (over 40,000 years ago), it's harder to pin down why. Some theories hold that people would mark the walls of caves to signal to others that the surrounding land was good hunting ground, or to conjure luck for an upcoming hunt; some assume that the images are meant to memorialize animals that had been sacrificed or killed, a way of assuring further prosperity; others hold that the animals—especially those inked deep in the caves' throats—were believed to be guides who helped religious leaders navigate into the spirit world and back again. While we can't ever *know* what these early paintings meant to those who composed them, from our perspective in the present the act of turning a living animal into an image is clearly and intimately related to death. Consider also: hunting map, elegy, spirit guide.

The present is dominated by elegy – no surprise, given that we are in the midst of a mass extinction. Scientists and artists alike have been obsessively documenting animals on their way out, often in the hopes of inspiring sympathy, outrage, and action. However, we suspect that these forms of documentation (the database, the list, the collage) tend instead to produce the feeling of being overwhelmed, to excise intimacy, to turn the animal – and, by extension, death – into data. While this may be necessary to imagine an ecopolitics that works on the scale of the global, that figures the human as just one endangered animal among many in order to reduce our hubris as a species, it ignores the way in which the all-too-human history of colonialism has made the relationship between human and non-human animal politically charged, particularly along the axes of race, ability, class, sexuality, and gender. How, that is, to ethically engage with the mass extinction of non-human animals when, at the same moment, we are faced with the mass murder of people, justified by a cultural imaginary in which these (black/brown/queer/crip) bodies have been rendered like-animal, and therefore disposable, available for consumption? It seems to us that answering this question requires inhabiting the image of the dead animal and working it for all of its possibilities, which necessarily involves charting the multiple intimacies, both literal and figurative, between human and non-human animals, in all of their violence, tenderness, melancholy, joy, and perversity. That is, this project is motivated by a deep interest in the power of images, their ability to act as forms of constraint and as vehicles for motion.

Rather than simply rejecting animality in order to claim humanity, many of these poems embrace the animal as a way of understanding the racialized, gendered, or sexual self, or in order to model forms of resistance. While these are old strategies, the increasing frequency of the public appearance of poems that use them is directly tied to the relatively recent increase in the presence and power of people who are not straightwhitemen in American letters.

The poems themselves were culled from writers who represent what many imagine to be distinct spheres: Pulitzer Prize Finalists, Community Organizers, National Poetry Slam Champions, National Book Award Winners, Cave Canem, and Kundiman Fellows. This time, instead of showcasing a particular community or school of poetry, in hunting dead animals across these various landscapes we were after poems that worked across assumed divisions, that devastated and stuffed and resurrected on the page, in the mouth, and in the ear all at once.

We'd like to thank University of Hell Press, to all of the writers who trusted us with their little undead machines, and to all of the books and journals in which these small gems have previously appeared.

We'd also like to thank you for picking up this weird field guide. May it be an escort through the menagerie of the stuffed and the sun bleached and the boiled, of the poisoned, and the putrid, and the soiled. May it serve all who turn to it be they extinct, newly dead, or not quite dead yet.

—*Cam Awkward-Rich* & *Sam Sax*

CONTENTS

Mass For Pentecost: Canticle For Birds & Waters – *D.A. Powell* 13

THE CANARY'S JOB IS TO DIE

[Untitled Work Poem] – *Corrina Bain* 17

Fiat Lux – *Traci Brimhall* 18

from Landscape With Saguaros – *Keith Ekiss* 19

When Edith Doesn't Have A Body – *Meg Freitag* 21

Per Fumum – *Jamaal May* 22

Hero(i)n – *Airea D. Matthews* 24

The Year Of Dead Geese – *Rachel McKibbens* 26

The Canary's Job Is To Die – *Lisa Olstein* 27

That Which Scatters And Breaks Apart – *Ladan Osman* 28

Sexton Texts From A Bird Conservancy – *Airea D. Matthews* 29

Theory Of Motion (3): The Sex Question – *Cam Awkward-Rich* 32

Swallow, Ducklings, Sugar Bowl – *Karrie Waarala* 34

SO FRESH THE GULLS HADN'T FOUND IT YET

Pounce – *Mark Bibbins* 39

Rain – *Brent Calderwood* 40

Letter From A Widowed Goldfish To Her
    Recently Departed Husband – *Jacob Dodson* 42

Wait – *Shira Erlichman* 43

Eastchester Bay [Ending With An Offering] – *Joey De Jesus* 44

Ruined – *Hieu Minh Nguyen*..45

Cheap Shot – *Layne Ransom*...46

Fishing – *Sam Sax*..47

UNTIL THE BARN IS EMPTY

Precipice – *Oliver Bendorf*..51

The Truth Of The Matter – *Sara Brickman*............................52

Cain – *Jericho Brown*...53

(Soma)Tic Poetry Ritual & Resulting Poem – *CAConrad*................54

Feed – *James Ellenberger*...56

How To Kill A Hog – *Rebecca Gayle Howell*...........................57

The Cow – *Michael McGriff*..60

O.S.R. – *Bill Moran*..65

EVERY DEAD DOG I EVER LOVED

Brown Noise – *Aziza Barnes*...71

Silence Unleashed – *Tara Betts*...73

Annie Mason's Collie – *Franny Choi*....................................74

Hunger – *Dominique Christina*..75

Love Is Like Walking The Dog – *Erich Haygun*.........................76

South – *Rachel McKibbens*..77

Laika – *Tomás Morin*...79

Unsent Replies To My Brother's
     Text Messages – *Sean Patrick Mulroy*..............................81

Exile The Dragon-Tailed And The
     Rabbit-Eared Among You – *Lisa Olstein*............................82

The Dogs And I Walked Our Woods – *Gretchen Primack*.................83

Fighters – *April Ranger*..84

Your Mother Says "I'm Just Surprised
     You're Not Angrier At Him, That's All" – *Jaz Sufi*................85

Hole In It – *Dean Young*...87

THE ANIMAL IN ME WANTS TO SEE
THE ANIMAL IN YOU

The Ghost Of The Author's Mother Has A Conversation
  With His Fiancée About Highways – *Hanif Willis-Abdurraqib* 91

Mosque In Galilee – *Kazim Ali* 93

Aubade For One Still Uncertain Of Being Born – *Meg Day* 94

Elegy For An Electrocuted Elephant – *Robin Ekiss* 95

from I Write To You From The Sea – *Laura Eve Engel* 97

Moose – *Joseph Legaspi* 99

Deer – *Deborah A. Miranda* 100

Tanning Process – *Christian Rees* 101

Juxtaposing The Road Kill & My Body – *Danez Smith* 103

Eurydice – *Ocean Vuong* 104

UNTIL THE MAGGOT IS KING OVER BODY

The Earthquake She Slept Through – *Mary Jo Bang* 109

Metamorphosis – *Malachi Black* 110

Aubade In Which The Bats Tried To Warn Me – *Traci Brimhall* 111

Better Than The Professionals – *Chen Chen* 113

My Heart Kicked Like A Mouse In A Paper Bag – *Martín Espada* 114

Aubade Ending With The Death Of A Mosquito – *Tarfia Faizullah* 116

Something About Joy – *Dinah Fay* 118

But First – *Carrie Fountain* 119

Promenade À Deux – *Meg Freitag* 121

Domestic Buildup – *Blake Lee Pate* 122

Ode To The White-Line-Swallowing Horizon – *Jamaal May* 123

Black Witch Moth – *Phillip B. Williams* 124

IN WHAT MANNER WE WILL JOIN THEM

Far North – *Scott Beal* 129

This Morning I Read The Wikipedia
Article For "Human" – *Emily Brown* 131

Want – *Eduardo Corral* 132

Dream With An Empty Chamber – *Aricka Foreman* 133

Carcass – *Tonya Ingram* 134

Ode To My Cat Euclid – *Noelle Kocot* 135

Self-Portrait, Wearing Bear Skull As Mask – *Michael Mlekoday* 136

Little Dead Wolves – *Jeremy Radin* 137

Haunted – *Naomi Shihab Nye* 138

Lady, That's A Lemur Get Out Of My Crotch – *Mary Alice Stewart* 139

Pitch For A Movie: Dinosaurs In The Hood – *Danez Smith* 141

Idaho – *Matthew Zapruder* 143

After – *Fatimah Asghar* 145

THE MANDIBLE AND THE LARVAL BROOD

Kings – *Nic Alea* 149

Motherhood: A Silk Scarf With
Hand-Painted Blood Hounds – *Lauren Berry* 151

No One Thinks Tools Are What Separates
Humans From Other Animals Anymore – *Daphne Gottlieb* 153

How To Make A Shadow – *Ladan Osman* 155

Petism – *Pubby* 157

Menagerie – *Austin Smith* 159

The Field – *David Winter* 161

Ica(sau)rus – *Jade Sylvan* 162

The Curse – *Jeananne Verlee* 163

MASS FOR PENTECOST:
CANTICLE FOR BIRDS & WATERS

There is no cause to grieve among the living or the dead,
>   so long as there is music in the air.

And where the water and the air divide, I'll take you there.
>   The levee aureate with yellow thistles.
White moth, wasp, and dragonfly.
>   We could not wish unless it were on wings.
Give us our means and point us toward the sun.

Will the spirit come to us now in the pewter paten of the air,
>   the fluted call of dabbler drakes, the deadpan honk
>   of the white-fronted goose, the tule goose.
Tongues confused in the matchstick rushes.
>   High, high the baldpate cries, and in the air,
and in the air, the red-winged blackbirds chase the damselflies.

Triumph over death with me. And we'll divide the air.

—D.A. POWELL

THE CANARY'S JOB IS TO DIE

Wherever the bird with no feet flew,
she found trees with no limbs
—Audre Lorde

[UNTITLED WORK POEM]

Some local sadist has found the corpse of a chickadee and hung it from a noose off of a lamppost. The reptile miracle of its feet scratching the air. Good morning. I am going to work, where I'll sit in a glass room and talk to a man, my father's age, about wanting to die. And he will tell me what I know, that he's wanted it before, that the medicine cabinet begins to growl a low, constant siren, the possibility before him like a lover he hasn't had in years. And while he's talking I will watch the jutting structures of his teeth, I will know that this is what my father has inside, beneath the obnoxious jokes and bluster, beyond me, because of course once you have a child you can't can't can't kill yourself, my uterus is folding over, too, vomiting blood onto a white bed. The last man who didn't want to sleep with me was like this, telling me no to keep from hurting me, as though I had not seen his grave around him, as if I were not asking to join him in it. Asking what city we're in, the day of the week, following the circuit of his breath, and he says it again. That there is no reason to keep doing this. I don't want to tell you what happens next. That I type his story and it floats, the bright white screen like a paper boat crossing a clear lake, over to a doctor who decides the cost and balance, that this man won't do it. That he'll live long enough to be sicker than this. The shock of seeing something hung from its neck, even when you know it can't have hung itself, even when you can claim, as I do, that it's not your fault.

—Corrina Bain

FIAT LUX

My sister asks what ate the bird's eyes
    as she cradles the dead chickadee she found
on the porch. *Ants,* I say, knowing the soft, ocular

cells are the easiest way into the red feast of heart,
    liver, kidney. I tell her that when they ate the bird
they saw the blue bowled sky, the patchwork

of soybean fields and sunflowers, a bear loping
    across a gravel road. Already, they are bringing
back to their tunnels the slow chapters of spring—

a slough drying to become a meadow and the bruised
    smell of sex inside flowers. They start to itch
for a mate's black-feathered throat and music.

As she cushions the eggs, their queen dreams
    of young chickadees stretching their necks and crying
for their mother to protect them until they learn to see.

Sister, it is like this—the visions begin to waver,
    and the colony goes mad, fearful they'll never see
another dahlia tell its purple rumor, or see a river commit

itself to the ocean. As the last memory leaves them,
    they twitch in their sleep, trying to make out the distant
boatman lifting his lantern, his face disfigured by light.

—TRACI BRIMHALL

from LANDSCAPE WITH SAGUAROS

Not even a heartbeat's needed to live.
The hummingbird on the ceiling beam
isn't dead or asleep. Blurry wings

snapped tight, a paper fan. To the bird
our house appears an accident—
flowerless aviary without any sugar.

My father, patient, climbs the ladder,
places the hummingbird's torpid body
in his palm, strokes the throat patch,

the gorget, muscle that should quiver.
Through an eyedropper, he feeds it
maraschino cherry juice. The dormant

heart accelerates, feathers hover,
he holds what I'm afraid to touch.

•

He killed what I'm afraid to touch.
The rattle sounds like camouflage—
mesquite pods shaken by wind.

I heard it ticking beneath the bed,
lost in the coolness of our house.
Better to find it flat, belly to dust,

the Bible says, not coiled like rope,
bullwhip lightning waits to strike.
My skin doesn't leave a hunting scent.

The carpet crawled with cruelty.
I recoiled. He slit the body lengthwise,
skinned it, hung the oily slough—

skeletal and waxy in garage light.
A warning if I think the desert's safe.

•

A warning if I think the desert's safe:
walking past the canal, I find a skull.
Hunter's quarry or hiker's gift?

It's light in my hand, not human.
Jawbone longer than the brain cavity,
teeth grist visible like fur.

Bone tissue flakes away as I rub it.
The skull isn't marble:
it's supple, closer to wood than stone.

By its teeth, I learn the animal name,
small for the pull of its ferocity.
I won't dislodge an eyetooth trophy—

I leave what's dead unshrouded.
Nothing that dies here needs burial.

—KEITH EKISS

WHEN EDITH DOESN'T HAVE A BODY

Edith can't hear me now
And neither can anyone else.
Nothing else to do with my fingers,
I shell pistachios into the red plastic cup
Someone left on the DVD player
During a party last week. I leave
The meats in a little pile
Beside the brass ashtray, like I would when Edith

Still had such a thing as an appetite, before
I started thinking about heaven
Like a two-way mirror laid down
For her to walk on. It's almost like
She just started flying but then didn't stop!
Except it didn't happen that way. Edith died
On the kitchen floor, halfway

Beneath the radiator. It took me an hour to find her.
And when I finally did I wanted to call to her,
In the other room, saying *Edith,*
I found her! I wanted to say to her
Edith, are you perched tightly? Because, shit,
This is going to break your heart.

—MEG FREITAG

PER FUMUM
Through Smoke

My mom became an ornithologist
the moment a grackle tumbled
through barbecue smoke
and fell at her feet. Later

she explained why singers cage birds;
it can take weeks for them to memorize
just one wayward melody,
since the first days are a wash, lost
as they mope and warble the friendless tone

every animal memorizes hours into breathing.
It's the knell a bottle of cologne would sound
if it were struck while something arcane
was aligned with a planet that was even more mythic
but farther away. My dad was an astronomer
for 20 minutes in a row
the first time a bus took us so far away
from streetlights he could see clearly,
point out constellations
that may or may not have been Draco,
Orion, Aquila, Crux. When they faded
I resented the sun's excess,
a combination of fires I couldn't even smell.

He told me the first chemist was a star perfumer.
Her combination for dizzy was brushed
against pulse points
so they could unlock when kissed

by quickening blood. From stolen perfumes
I concocted a toxin I could call my own
but learned it was no more deadly
than that amount of water
to any creature the size of a roach.
I grew suspicious of my plate and lighter
Bunsen burner, the tiny vials accumulating
in my closet. I was a chemist for months
before I learned the difference
between poisoned and drowned.
When my bed caught fire
it smelled like a garden.

—JAMAAL MAY

HERO(i)N

I thought it was a bird. Skimmed rush. Hush as before a fowl fixes

    its head up from shadow water

sickened by its own nature, narcissus-

           reversed. unfortunate predatory

consequence. the luck. heron spots two ducklings nesting on an outcrop

    of rocks.

Swift-like. heron bounces off the lake, a hollowed pebble. in one swallow

    babes go

down. pulsing inside heron's throat until they succumb. mama

      mallard squawks and plods—helpless, she flies low

away. how long do mother ducks mourn—until the next day

      next month, until pitch pines
shake barren

    or a naked beggar shakes on his kitchen floor like

breccia in a rain stick, begging: *2 bird bags, 4 quarters, 1 gram?* His daughters

    empty cupboards, offer open tin at his feet—*eat, eat*—until

    heron comes.   when sick,

fowl fit in veins like ducks in necks—vortex of sorts.

some knew this.

yet, none bothered to explain how
hero(i)n
made him fly

why hero(i)n

made him
well, less starved.

—AIREA D. MATTHEWS

THE YEAR OF DEAD GEESE

Ghost flock—you,
slick with gasoline—what
cruel boys could have done this?
Your feathers crippled black and
heavy. Necks turned. Slender bills
crushed by feet that came like stones.
I am mad, still. My hair is wild
with it. We carried you
in buckets, laid you out
on trash bags as our teacher,
a man of science, wept for God.
Your stained flight gone quiet
and flammable. The police
came with cameras and
rubber gloves. But we
children, not yet as wicked
as other children chose to be,
washed you
with our bare hands,
heavied our flesh
with blood and oil.
The wingless left behind;
when they buried you,
they buried us, too.

—RACHEL McKIBBENS

THE CANARY'S JOB IS TO DIE

little flame
little match struck

little sunspot
little filament

golden smudge
silent siren

of no more air
of no longer there

suddenly fled we flee
go ahead and try

go ahead and die

—LISA OLSTEIN

THAT WHICH SCATTERS AND BREAKS APART

Everywhere they turn, the walls ask, *why, why not.*
From every space someone calls a question
and there echoes so many answers, it's impossible to hear.

Save me, he calls.
Open me, she calls. *Divorce me.*
Their despair is a bird in an abandoned nest,
its brother has jumped out and died, its sister is dying beside it
and still it perches:
Do I fly?
Can I fly?

You're here because you said,
I hate you instead of, *I'm sorry.*
You're here because you couldn't forgive
but kept on making stews and hand-washing his good socks,
blowing curses into hot water.

—LADAN OSMAN

SEXTON TEXTS FROM A BIRD CONSERVANCY

Fri, July 2, 7:07 pm
"Eat, the stones a poor man breaks,"

Fri, July 2, 7:18 pm
It was 27 springs ago
when grandmother died,
half-mad on working class
hunger; plumpness thinned
to a chip of lamb's bone,
legs decayed, necrotic;

Fri, July 2, 7:26 pm
Running is a game
for the young. Women
of a certain age, root.

Fri, July 2, 9:09 pm
I was her deep-water Chola,
dreamy eyed peacock,
temperamental spunforce
bladefeather.

Fri, July 2, 9:11 pm
Can you believe I still carry
the knife my mother left me?
I gut, hollow, and scrape
soft rot from cavities, but. . .

Fri, July 2, 9:21 pm
The dead are pretty well empty.
Makes for easy work, no?
My kin deal in full-ghost metal
jackets. No one knows
what's in the chamber,
staring down our barrels.

Fri, July 2, 9:32 pm
There's 2 ways to terrify men:
tell them what's coming,
don't tell them what's next. . .

Fri, July 2, 9:54 pm
(1/2) pales lower on deathbeds
Memaw saw all varieties
of birds hovering—

Fri, July 2, 9:55 pm
(2/2)in trees,
mid-air, her room, overhead
vultures, peregrine falcons, white-
winged blackbirds, mute cygnus,
Impundulu. . .

Fri, July 2, 10:07 pm
What did Impundulu want?

Fri, July 2, 10:10 pm
Wondered myself. She named
uncles, aunts, and gods I'd never
met—
Osiris in Brooks Brothers, Isis in
Fredrick's of Hollywood, polyester-
clad Jesus.

Fri, July 2, 10:13 pm
Ah, the birds wanted them then.

Fri, July 2, 10:17 pm
No. She said: *They waitin'...
for you*.
And then she died,
eyes wide,
fixed on me

Fri, July 2, 10:28 pm
Dinn, dinn, dinn—
Dying's last words
mean nothing. What wants you
dead would have you dead.

Fri, July 2, 10:29 pm
LOL! But I'm not dead, huh?

Fri, July 2, 11:21 pm
I'm not, right?

Sat, July 3, 1:07 am
Anne, Anne, are you still there?
I'm not, right?

—AIREA D. MATTHEWS

THEORY OF MOTION (3): THE SEX QUESTION

Do people who like sex have a question about it too?
        —Anne Carson, *The Autobiography of Red*

The only words I have to explain it
are not the kind anyone wants to hear—
You look just like a headless chicken, darling
or *I love the way you are so like a puppet
made of meat. How I can slip my hand inside
& make you sing sweet & just for me.*

Ok, maybe the headless chicken thing
needs further explanation—

Tonight, I want you to pluck the bird
from my throat. To be the dumb singing
animal. I want to watch you change
behind your eyes & pull feathers
from your teeth.

See, I do want to learn to leave my body
without blood. So maybe *headless
chicken* is the wrong image after all.
Maybe it's more like *woodpecker
in a room made of glass.* Maybe
my question is—what does it feel like
to be thrown wide open? & where do you go
once I've shattered all the windows
once there's nothing left to beat
your wings against but the red
air outside?

Tonight, I want you to train me to fly.

That's better, right? To call it *flight*
& not *the meat's idiot dance once the boy
has left the building*? Me, I've wanted
to be a thousand things. I've got names
for all of them & as many kinds
of travel—the knife, the needle, the wolf
in bird's clothes.

So I say *take me* & I mean *darling, teach me
to dance from the wet ruins of myself.* I mean
*I have a question, an image, a feathered head
in my mouth.*

—CAM AWKWARD-RICH

SWALLOW, DUCKLINGS, SUGAR BOWL

1.

A shimmering tuft of blue and brown feathers
nestles in the gloved cup of my hands
and I hesitate to even breathe lest I break
the beady gaze cocked sideways at me over beak,
this long moment of trust braided to fear.

I know I am not supposed to handle wild birds.
But its desperate flutter nabbed my attention
from the barn floor where the hooves
of ten hungry horses churned the dust and I
swooped in to scoop it to safety.

The stillness of little shell heart hammering
against my palm flurries to an end in panicked wings,
and I hurry to tuck the creature out of reach just
until the snorting hulks are fed and turned out.

When I return, my tiny responsibility is dead.

2.

I try to console myself by thinking that at least I
am not the monster plastered across the local news,
the thug high on being impervious and nineteen
and privileged enough to own a Hummer,
a snorting hulk he uses to deliberately crush

four fuzzed infants wobbling around a parking lot.
They're everywhere lately, you know, since it's been

a relentless curtain of rain for weeks now and even
McDonald's asphalt dipped and curved enough to
cup puddles must seem reasonable to a mother

trying to tuck her tiny flurry of responsibilities
somewhere safe, somewhere sensible, and I just
keep wondering how she grieved after a roar
of rubber and exhaust and maliciousness

churned half of her brood into the pavement.

3.

For three years' worth of mornings I have thought
through the fuzzed pre-coffee cloud that I should
really get rid of this thing, this ugly kitchen necessity
that was never meant to be mine, that has outlasted
my grief, that didn't move out when he did.

This squat bit of glass has poked relentlessly at
memory's malicious bruise, and I wonder why
I haven't replaced it sooner, what made yesterday
the moment to casually add something simple and new
and mine to the shopping cart, how impervious the sound

of it being crushed against pavement would make me.
But enough fragile things have been broken today.
Instead, I cup it in my hands one last time,
nestle it into the trash can much the way earlier

I laid to rest the tiny corpse still lovely in my palm.

—KARRIE WAARALA

SO FRESH THE GULLS HADN'T FOUND IT YET

Having already in various ways put before you his skull, spout-hole, jaw, teeth, tail, forehead, fins, and diverse other parts, I shall now simply point out what is most interesting in the general bulk of his unobstructed bones.
—Herman Melville

POUNCE

He's the prettiest thing I've ever seen/
synthetic boy/imploding star.
You can't swing a dead fish

and expect to split the dissonance.
An ego unhinged by chemicals/
the prettiest thing I've ever seen.

The seconds commiserate and pounce/
oh I am but a simple tramp I know/
in underground rivers forgotten fish

glow. I've seen a future there
in the skittish projections/his eye
the prettiest eyes I've ever seen.

He slid down a mountain of steel
to drop his bread in the sea
and I went to where the fish

return before they replicate and die.
I would ask no more of the world/
the prettiest thing I've ever seen
flattens my heart like scales on a fish.

—MARK BIBBINS

RAIN

Here comes the rain again.
The tsunami came to Japan yesterday
and five thousand miles to the east,
the bay is huge, swaying and gray,
an elephant butting its head into the dunes.
When the plovers come back tomorrow,
they'll perforate the sand in neat little rows,
searching for whatever it is plovers eat.

I want to walk in the open wind.
But it's coming so hard I have to hold
my umbrella like a riot shield,
the metal legs straining in the squall.
I should pick up a phone. I should call
my sister-in-law. She lost her husband on Friday.
I should call my mother, who lost one of her sons
but who does that anymore—pick up a phone, I mean?
We carry them with us.

I want to talk like lovers do.
The night of the election
I was missing your big kitchen,
the seasoned pan, that trick you taught me
for cutting onions. The next morning
it was like the poster said, HOPE—
I even thought of calling you,
even forgot about the marriage amendment.
My family didn't—think to call, I mean.
No one said "It's not fair."

I want to dive into your ocean.
In the video, Annie Lennox
is walking into the sea like Virginia Woolf,
or, if that was a river, then like James Mason
at the end of *A Star is Born*.
MTV wouldn't play her at first—
Annie Lennox, I mean—
they said she looked too much like a man.

Is it raining with you?
Last week I saw a seal pup wash onto the shore,
a black purse spilling open with opals, rubies,
so fresh the gulls hadn't found it yet—
they were still squawking downwind
round a crab, and when I came close they flew off.
Their feet had scratched out a wreath of little Vs,
three rows deep, each pointing out from the middle,
away from the ticking thing,
half-eaten, half-alive.

—BRENT CALDERWOOD

LETTER FROM A WIDOWED GOLDFISH TO HER RECENTLY DEPARTED HUSBAND

Who?

—Jacob Dodson

WAIT

Fifteen stories up and I could smell it. Who knows where it came from.
They found it stranded on the shore, but the neighbors say the sky
brought it. It smelled like quarters and its grey skin shone silver
where it was wet. I watched them from my window, fifteen stories up.
They were dressed all in white. Clouds of dust rose from the moving
of feet. Then, as if it had been filled with firecrackers, the whale exploded.
A huge roar let out. White clothes turned red. A strand of guts,
deep purple, dangled from a lamppost. The whale, no longer in one piece,
could not be carried. Soon, night came, and with that, the street cleaners.
My father is one of them. He continues to go out and sweep, even though
they have long since let him go. Tonight, he comes home with purple hands.
"I brought you something," he says. "You've been drinking again," I say.
He leans in and his breath smells like danger. "That whale refused to go out
softly," he says. Something inside my father's eyes. I can see it flick its tail
out of the water. "This is for you," he hands me a tooth. It is curved like a comma
as if our bodies were built of waiting. "You smell like gin," I say. He kisses
the top of my head, walks towards his bedroom. Around midnight I get up
for a drink of water and check on him and it has happened. I do not think.
I put on my shoes. I step outside. The night is black and warm. I walk the streets,
trying to clean them of his blood, his breath. But everything is clean. I feel the tooth
in my pocket. It says, Stop. For what, I say, and it echoes. Something invisible
sets off a car alarm. All I can do is stand in the middle of the dark street and wait.

—Shira Erlichman

EASTCHESTER BAY [ENDING WITH AN OFFERING]

Now to waterscape; I am escaping.
Now to hooking bunker in the stern,

the cooler full with bluefish flop,
the forearm sequined in broodspewn scale,

and here stands I   darting minnows
fishing with my child in our porgy spot

who tails angling boys, thinks
bait & tackle—the sea did good

to starve him alive. The tongue did fix
to good filet knife—Two-fingered spirit

of trawling gut, I will give him back.
I will teach him how a single line

beleaguers dark water,
whose fiend soul is bigger than us all.

—JOEY DE JESUS

RUINED

It's not bad luck to name your goldfish
after the goldfish that has already died,

right? It seems impossible, on days like this,
to walk to work and not daydream

of ways to make eye contact
with people wearing sunglasses.

It usually involves tripping or love.
My mother never told me the *no glove* rule,

just hung photographs of dead relatives
in the living room and photos of herself

in my bedroom. One day, if I'm lucky
enough to outlive her, I will pick the photo

with the perm—she fears this the most—
that, and having a son ruined by want,

by endless limbs of other sons.
My mother never told me about the first boy

I was named after—just said he died
in a desert, just said he lost his way.

She flushed my old body down the toilet,
then took my photo off the wall.

—Hieu Minh Nguyen

CHEAP SHOT

The moon admires a modernist painting, other deeply
annoying things happen, etc. Most of my spiritual experiences
involve a fried food drizzled with some other food
and one or more of those foods is purposefully dead.
Like, a person killed an animal, not suicide, though sometimes
those things happen, like when whole whale families
just give up and die together on a bright, pretty beach.

—LAYNE RANSOM

FISHING

we stole fish from the ocean,
butchered, threw them back in pieces
on hooks. the two of us: me and daniel with grease in his hair
on a dock that reached out
        into the water like a man with broken arms
wood rotting in his arms. daniel
   with well oiled hair,   with a throat like a lighthouse, with a mouth
like black water. sometimes i think all he was
        was eyes. the kind that roll up into the skull
like a map   that will burn before they show you   water.

fish don't have throats to cut, so we stabbed
        wildly. my first knife, bright as a smile, sectioned their seizing
bodies. my smile, my knife.
                daniel and i.   worked with no care
  for their anatomy, for the proper way to make them
open. perhaps, our forearms touched
        as guts spilled into our upturned palms
as we slid hooks through their skins
          as we threw them back in
and pulled out fish that looked just like them
          as if the ocean had pieced them back together.

that night we slept
        in his mother's house. in the dark, i ran my fingers through
his hair, brought them to my face and tasted salt.

i wanted so badly
        to be a knife then. to take him
apart in pieces. to throw him back
                in the ocean.

or perhaps, i wanted to take him
       into my mouth, to feel something sharp
break inside of me,
          to be pulled up
              into the screaming air,
                   somehow whole.

—SAM SAX

UNTIL THE BARN IS EMPTY

Silently the animal catches our glance. The animal looks at us, and whether we look away (from the animal, our plate, our concern, ourselves) or not, we are exposed.
—Jonathan Safron Foer

PRECIPICE

I don't farm for milk. I farm for the front row
      seat to things living and dying. The dead bird

            like a small wet sock in a cement crack
    behind the barn, crawling with hungry worms.

The goats' voices changing from high whinny
      to pubescent music box and then to western

           station just below the dial. I farm not for
    the countryside but for the tumbling sense inside me

that everything has to transform eventually. My
      masculinity is animal at best: bellowing hoot

           of a barred owl. The wren dad's song.
    Wethers who will stay boys forever. There are a million

and one ways for me to look, but I only want one.
I teeter at the edge.

—OLIVER BENDORF

THE TRUTH OF THE MATTER

I don't know how many ribs I ate
but some animal had to die for me to have each one
and you're a rapist,
no matter what you say.
If you want truth to be objective so badly
doesn't your reality have to intersect with mine at least a little?
Doesn't your heart have to fall apart in the slaughterhouse
sluice just like any other person? I get it,
it hurts to learn you've been operating
a roadside attraction where girls get moved to strange
cities on the promise of love
and end up with apples in their mouths
and a souvenir t-shirt they get to keep.

But I promise you it doesn't feel
like having your body mapped
for the juiciest cuts. I promise
it doesn't feel like looking in the eyes of the butcher
his hand stroking your neck softly
while he holds you down on the block
whispering sugar before the knife comes down
shushhh you're safe here. Sweet creature, you're
safe.

—SARA BRICKMAN

CAIN

First, a conversation. Now,
A volcano. Call me quick-
Tempered vegan. Turnip
Lover. Fruit licker. Mound
Maker. Quiet. I can predict
An earthquake. I can cook
A rose. I'm first to kill
A weed. The collards
Should come quick this year.
The beans may be lean.
plant seeds and wait
All winter to eat. Some
laughter sheep for dinner.
Some chew leaves. Firstborn
And patient, I give ground
Color. Pull pink from
Green. Azalea, vibrant
As a lamb's tongue. My kid
Brother killed one, but I
Dug the hole, soil still
Young, lava beneath it
Near each finger when little
Brothers tortured most
Of God's creatures, and small
Men watched them bleed.

—JERICHO BROWN

(SOMA)TIC POETRY RITUAL & RESULTING POEM

TAROT AS VERB
TAROTING MEAT

—for Selah Ann Saterstrom

"I saw you, sister, standing in this brilliance."
—Paul Celan

Seeking potential conversations with the dead in grocery stores? Lacking the respect of a churchyard, stacks of chopped bodies wrapped in plastic and styrofoam, stamped with dates and prices, the refrigerator is not the grave the human stomach is the grave. Grocery store refrigerators are like any morgue awaiting someone to claim the body. Take a deep breath, close your eyes and listen. There is a particular and very noticeable chatter beneath the clear plastic shrouds, making the listener enter a quiet, cold meditation. Stand before the hacked animal joints, stomach and shoulder fat, and cut the tarot deck nine times, then read the cards.

Memories stored in flesh all flesh all humans and other animals on the prairie, by the bay, in the city, or incarcerated in prisons or zoos (which are prisons built to amuse children and their nescient parents). Memories of joy and suffering, anyone who has received extensive massage or acupuncture knows the body can release feelings long secluded in muscle and other tissue. It's a glorious thing such freedom. Give this to grocery store animals with their fur ripped away, their tongues removed, their bones cracked and sawed from ligaments. Pull the cards, pull them, see how they walked and felt the touch of sunlight. Unfetter a bit of the pain. One, two, three cards pulled for chops, roasts, and hamburger patties. Take notes about love you have known for those who were shown none. Notes from taroting at the display of conformist serial killing will become a poem, another communiqué, one for humans loosening their impediments of ignorance of suffering.

EQUIVOCATORS THRU A GREASY

wrong

door to wrong step
costs so
little no
one will

notice eating wings in divergent flight
if gossip is poetry
I'm out of here
side arms
extend back to
planetary spinning as
another punctured forehead with
old habits dangles in
miniature salt water vase
parrot sleeping in
tome of his
story
though it was
her story
tears taste
exactly the
same all
over the
world god damn

—CACONRAD

FEED

it bleeds hard into the tub / I clipped the windpipe

I didn't mean to / I'm careless with a razor

I bleed on Sundays and walk / into church a man

from the desert / I walk in with bloodsmell

I wear it as the women / wear feathers in their hats

I'll dry its bones / on flood-flat stones

dried bones are a wrecked boat / I stuck it alive

pig heart thumping the moon / wide wound a tide

in the throat / it hung from a beam like a pear

a pair of black eyes / the buttons on the pastor's cuffs

he sings glory I sing hallelujah / the chariot the cross

the pig's heart / in a rain pan on my porch

—James Ellenberger

HOW TO KILL A HOG

Do you remember how close
you were to her

when she was farrowing
and she needed you

her bawling drawing
you out of bed

a bad dream
how you washed her vulva, soft

warm water over your own
hands how you scrubbed

even your fingernails
under your fingernails

before you came to the pen and the sun-
flower oil you coated yourself in

so she would not chafe
even as she hemorrhaged

and how against all this
bloody shit and hay

you took each piglet
out of her night and into yours

into your palm and cleared
its mouth its nose of mucus

how you brought breath
to each set of tiny lungs

how you washed
how you opened her

That is how to touch her now

Once she is hung
and cut straight cut

from rectum to neck
while the other men

take their cigarettes
find quick coffee, food

Lag behind wait
until the barn is empty

until you are alone
Then step inside her

your arms inside her
death like it is a room

your private room
peculiar and clean

Gather her organs up
into your arms

like you once did your mother's robes
when you were a boy who knew nothing

but the scent of sweat and silk
Hold her and inhale

Before reaching all the way around
to snip the last tendon

before you cut the stomach
intestines kidney liver

before you cut her heart
out

and she drops into you
and drops down

into the cold wash tub
of this day

close your eyes just once
just once

do not look away

—REBECCA GAYLE HOWELL

THE COW

I used to think of this creek as a river
springing from mineral caverns
of moonmilk and slime,

but really it's just a slow thread of water
that comes from somewhere up north
to trickle its way out
near the edge of our property.

And I've always imagined
the tool shed as it is,
though it was once
an outbuilding for a watermill
whose wheel and timbers
have been reborn
as exposed rafters and flooring
for the Old Money in the valley.

The day before my grandfather died
he drove a diesel flatbed
to the edge of the creek
and paid ten day laborers
to unload this shed.

He left his will on the shed floor,
which wasn't a will
as much as it was a quick note
scrawled on the pink edge of an invoice
for a few bundles of chicken wire.

I found the note
and showed it to no one.

This shed should have the smell
of seed packets and mouse traps.
It should have a calendar
whose pages haven't turned since Truman.

The sounds of usefulness and nostalgia
should creak from its hinges,
but instead there's nothing
but a painting the size of a dinner plate
that hangs from an eight-penny nail,
a certain style of painting
where the wall of a building
has been lifted away
to reveal the goings-on of each room,
which, in this case, is a farm house
where some men and women
sit around the geometry
of a kitchen table playing pinochle,
a few of the women laughing
a feast-day kind of laughter
and one of the men, a fat one
in overalls with a quick brushstroke
for a mouth, points up
as if to say something
about death or the rain
or the reliable Nordic construction
of the rafters.

A few of the children
gathered in a room off to one side
have vaguely religious faces—
they're sitting on the floor around their weak
but dependable uncle
who plays something festive
on the piano. The piano
next to the fireplace, the fireplace lit,
a painting of the farmhouse
hanging above the mantel.

What passes for Middle C
ripples away from the uncle, the children,
the pinochle game—
the wobbling note finally collapsing
in the ear of the cow
standing in perfect profile
at the far right of the painting.

The cow faces east and stands knee-deep
in pasture mud. The pasture
is a yellow, perspectiveless square,
and the cow, if you moved her
inside the house, would stand
with the sway of its back
touching the rafters.
Perhaps the fat man is referring
to the impossibility of it all,
the inevitable disproportion,
the slow hiss of something he can't explain.

The cow is gray and blue
and orange. This is the cow
that dies in me every night,
the one that doesn't sleep
standing up, or sleep at all,
but stamps through the pasture muck
just to watch the suckholes she makes
fill with a salty rot-water
that runs a few inches
below the surface of everything here.

The cow noses through
the same weak spot in the same fence,
and every night finds herself
moving out beyond the field of its dumb,
sleeping sisters.

The cow in me has long admired
the story the night tells itself,
the one with rifle shots and laughter,

gravel roads crunching under pickups
with their engines and lights cut,
the story with the owls
diving through the circles
their iron silences
scratch into the air.

The cow in me never makes it past
the edge of the painting—
and she's not up to her knees in mud,
she's knee-deep in a cattle guard.
Bone and hoof and hoods of skin
dangle below the steel piping
into the clouds of the underworld.

The cow cries, and its cry
slits the night open and takes up house.
The cry has a blue interior
and snaps like a bonfire stoked
with dry rot and green wood.

The cry is a pitcher of ink that never spills,
until it does, until it scrawls itself
across the fields and up into the trees.

The cry works in the night
like a dated but efficient system.

The cry becomes a thread of black water
where the death-fish spawn.

On nights like this
the cow inside me cries
and I wake as the cry leaves my mouth
to find its way back to the shed,
where it spreads
through all the little rooms of the painting
like the heat building up
from the woodstove by the piano.

The cry makes a little eddy
around the fat man's finger.

It turns the pinochle deck
into the sounds of the creek
trickling into nothing.

The cry watches my grandfather
weeping over the only thing
he said to my father
in two decades,
which he didn't say at all
but penned onto a crumpled invoice
that found its way to the nowhere
of my hands.

The cry in the cow
in the painting in me
rotates in the night
on a long axle of pain,
and the night itself
has no vanishing point.

—MICHAEL MCGRIFF

O.S.R.

I.
Dandelion:
from the French for "the lion's tooth."
But we already know this—
how bones break
easily.

II.
First the bull, then Bourbon Street.
Come morning, we'll be gone. But first,
we have to bury this goddamn bull.

Your pop's most expensive steer, Simon, died of a virus.
Alright so, we did what we had to do:
bought rope, and beer, hitched him to your truck by his hind legs, and toasted
a six pack each to some dead animal.
At dawn, we'll drag his body out to the clearing where the grass is green
and the dandelions are bone.

Easy.
If you've ever eaten painkillers without counting 'em first,
you can bury a bull.
It's the same thing—
you leave it in the grass
and let it sink.
Dragging it out there's harder.
Like last time, it was a nice march.
A Mardi Gras of cattle, cows, and calves second-lining behind your Ford,
brass hides and horns
polished to a sheen,

tuba and trombone heads hung,
blaring off-key for Simon
(as if cattle could wail, right?
As if funeral is something that happens to us, easy as laugh or yawn.
As if "Bye And Bye" could parade-float up out a calf's belly.
As if grief were milk.)

The grass was the jaw of a tuba.
We untied the bull, left him there,
and headed for New Orleans.

III.
On Bourbon Street, you
have a hand grenade belly, your belt tied around your forehead
like it's holding you together, slack end hanging—a horn of faux leather, aimed
at the earth,
when you get the news:

           your brother's dead.
You loosen the belt. Your head falls clean off the bone.

In Texas, I help you tie your heart to your truck's hitch,
and we follow your little brother's hearse
to the cemetery,
smearing your heart on Old San Antonio Road
like sick livestock
until it's either a handful of dandelions or bones, I don't know.

I take a bite and find out.
And again, I dream that I am the grass.
Grief grows up from my belly.
Little bulls walk on my grief field, grazing.
Again, the bulls wail:
"Let go or be dragged. Let go or be dragged."

IV.
Friend,
again and again we have watched cattle sink into East Texas

and now we know
that god is bone.
Indeed, we have dragged our god so far,
all that's left is the bone;
even that's chipping off.
We call it "dandelion" or some white flower—
I don't know,
anything that'll grow back.

One of these days, Bourbon Street will go white with dandelions
and we will go there to die.
We who lead our hearts to the Bull's Teeth by the hand.
We who graze on your brother's first name,
our breakfast of grass,
and eat his cufflinks, his boutonniere, the white flowers right out of his white
hands.
Our wax eyes we do not close.
We know how easy the wax melts.
We know it is not milk, it is hot,
yet I lap it off your cheek anyway
and barhop to the Minotaur's front door and black out.
Our Grief is a red cape.
Us bulls, we dance like this
and call it Whygod.
Grief is the virus,
the medicine is More.

It's too goddamn hot to bury a kid today
but we do it.

Hitch up your heart, your Sunday best, your father by his leg
and drive.
Dillon, this is the tax we are to pay and we pay it.
Us weeds don't know how to die, yeah,
but we do it
anyway.
We do what we have to do:

       hand in our coins

and brothers,

keep a straight face,

act sober.

V.
A very thirsty Heaven beg us to sink into it
    but in Texas, there's always another bull to bury

    first.

—Bill Moran

EVERY DEAD DOG I EVER LOVED

*The dog, we realize, though he is old
and has lost his sight, can always tell
when a ghost is about*
—Kathryn Bond Stockton

BROWN NOISE

We are a fifth
of Hennessy & here. Sticky

fingertips, strays emerging
from under cars at this 5am. You

staring at my chest, me staring at
smaller animals. *Y'all don't keep*

y'all dogs on leashes? I say &
see anyway. They don't bite. I know you

are going to ask me about my lips,
the mouth behind them. How did they meet?

How did they stay? I know you are going
to leave me, 1/2 naked & barking. I know

you are going to drive me to a street without a name & spit
on the tender of my thigh. I know I am only one

name you've forgotten. *I want to tear them,*
you say. I am staring at a dog, her teats dragging

on the gravel. I am tired like that. *How?*
You're in my pants, rooting for an angle of them & I

am laughing. *With your teeth?* I'm picturing you
gnawing at their matte lace, rabid the way pleasure

sickens us. Your hands still. My mouth is wet
& closed. Then the rip, crisp as new money. They're

dangling long, hanging by whatever
thread is left. *Do you put your dogs in the pound*

if they bite? I know you are staring
at them, the cross- hatching of your

shred, me: a tremor of meat made more
naked. *No,* you say. *We shoot them.*

—AZIZA BARNES

SILENCE UNLEASHED

Watch them throw the dead Doberman
by the legs into the garbage truck's open
hull. Watch the still body join trash bags,
broken chairs, candy wrappers, stray bottles.
Watch the men fling the body. Remember
the dog's sleek black warmth under your
small hands. Sheba would come when her
name was called and bow her narrow head.
She hears nothing, and all that's left is
the roar of the truck in your ears. Let
the curtain drop silently from unclamped
knuckles. Try to forget what you don't hear.

—TARA BETTS

ANNIE MASON'S COLLIE

was the first death she watched.
In the kitchen
the dog lifted its head
before its body emptied
quiet as a sink.

I've never seen death
streak across the sky
of a loved one's face—
just mapped out the craters it leaves

stayed up with dreams
of its explode and
howl and nothing
clogging my eyes. I am

lucky.

     Annie married
her letter jacket love
last winter. Sometimes it all
works out. I kept the invitation
on my dresser for months.

Let it curl
first into bark   then ash.

—FRANNY CHOI

HUNGER

right at dawn i could hear that damn dog
scratching at the fence,
a forever howl soliloquy
to tell about the hunger.

i went out one day,
being feral and starved   myself,
climbed the gate
and struck it with a rock.
its mouth shingle-loose
the tongue snatched bloody and limp.
killing and killing the siren call of want.
simple.

I'm the one who is hungry bitch. ME.

—Dominique Christina

LOVE IS LIKE WALKING THE DOG

Sometimes you don't want to
& wonder why you ever wished
            this responsibility into existence

When the act of keeping can be its own cruelty
            & anything adorable is also a little annoying

Still you know it is not a chore you can avoid
            for long   Picking up shit
            left behind is your entire life

Even when the weather's terrible
            Even if the dog is dead

—ERICH HAYGUN

SOUTH

We were driving down I-90 from Ohio.
All five of the kids crammed in the back seat
with a cooler full of sandwiches. We'd been
driving in silence most of the way;
there wasn't any music the seven of us
could agree on. It was a long stretch.
New York August hot.
I saw a blue truck pull over about a mile
up the road. The driver got out and opened
the passenger-side door to let out his dog.
A big Golden Retriever with a red handkerchief
tied around his neck.
Instead of running towards the field
the dog rushed across three lanes of traffic,
then cut a left into mine. I had nowhere to steer.
Cars on my right. A ditch to my left.
My children in the backseat. I didn't have a choice.
That goddamn dog. Ran up my lane.
Charging. So fast. Excited. As if he were running home.
My oldest son became the only thing I could feel.
He spoke to me steadily. Calm. It's okay, mom.
There's nothing else you can do. Close your eyes.
It's okay.
A brief impact. Solid. I closed my eyes
for maybe two seconds. I don't want to tell you
where I went in that time. The house on South Street.
Three hours past curfew. When your uncle came
into your bedroom. And he walked over
to the pink transistor radio. And instead of turning it off,

he turned it up. And when he stood over us
in our sleeping bags, the look that he gave us.
My god, there is nothing else in the world
                                like it.

—RACHEL MCKIBBENS

LAIKA

In '57 Sputnik 2 carried her into space
where the first bark went unheard.
Did she lick herself or nip at the whir
of the fan in that cabin? These concerns
were not important to science, unlike velocity,
heart rate, time of death. When my faith
in justice wavers I embrace my inner Greek
and butcher the sky, carve out a swath of stars
catching a curve of light millions of years old
and pretend they are the outline of a dog,
half husky, half terrier. I retreat to this fantasia
when another report of animal cruelty
soils further the already filthy news.
It was years before we knew
she didn't last more than five hours
in that wretched kennel, weightless,
and think of the trash she could have rooted,
the black boots she could have shined
with a few well-placed curtsies
in deference to the great mutts of history—
think Khrushchev and Kennedy.
Sweet Laika, it has been decades since my last confession,
and my sins are many: in Kathmandu I herded strays
through the alleys, ticked their foreheads
and paws red, wept in gratitude when they licked my face
because now they might let me pass
through the gates of heaven with only a tender snarl
for having diced garlic, may the bulbs forgive me,
in the kitchens of Laos. I went my whole life
without seeing a dog struck by a car and then it was there—
have mercy upon the pronoun, I didn't get out—

in the mirror, watching the Chevys and Fords,
pounding the pavement with its tail before the truck
hauling from Georgia who knows what,
and it was in that other Georgia, the colder one,
where I entered the life of a minor scientist,
hunting the bakeries of Moscow for tea cake
one day, the trash heaps the next for any dog
the size of a breadbox, one not much bigger
than the tabby at the foot of my bed dreaming
about the injustice of wings, unaware of my past
allegiances, that I was born under the sign of the dog,
that I have lived and died a traitor to my own kind.

—TOMÁS MORIN

UNSENT REPLIES TO MY BROTHER'S TEXT MESSAGES

there's a headless dog in the back yard
running circles in the grass.

a cloud of flies spews from its open neck.
its filthy coat
mud colored,
shivering with wings.

its fat feet tearing up the yard,
arcs of its blood and piss flood from its holes,
spill into the garden.

no one can remember
where the dog came from,
what it used to be like before something
stole its head.

I don't understand. without a mouth how can it eat?
how does it survive?
why is it still here?
it's sick, the sound of scratching at the door.
I think it wants something inside the house
I think it wants someone to touch it
with their hands.
My god, it thinks someone is going to love it.

—Sean Patrick Mulroy

EXILE THE DRAGON-TAILED AND THE RABBIT-EARED AMONG YOU

There is a queen peeking
from your bedroom window
as if a terrace, as if a crowd.
Nobody notices her waving
in the dark. She didn't ask for this
life. Yellow was chosen for her
six hundred years ago during
a short truce in a long war.
Every dog I ever loved just died,
say her eyes as the eyes of every
dead dog I ever loved stare back at me
from the windowsill and earlier
at the check-out counter as the clerk
explained how carefully he crushed
between two spoons the pills
into a fine powder, stirred them
into a bowl of meat and carried Pal
outside for one last meal. Maybe
you're in trouble, says the queen.
Maybe you don't need a lover.
Maybe you're a thousand ways broken.

—LISA OLSTEIN

THE DOGS AND I WALKED OUR WOODS

and there was a dog, precisely the colors of autumn,
asleep between two trunks by the trail.
But it was a coyote, paws pink
with a clean-through hole in the left,
and a deep hole in the back of the neck,
dragged and placed in the low crotch
of a tree. But it was two coyotes,
the other's hole in the side of the neck,
the other with a dried pool of blood below
the nose, a dried pool below the anus,
the other dragged and placed
in the adjoining low crook, the other's body
a precise mirror of the first. The eyes were closed,
the fur smooth and precisely the colors
of autumn, a little warm to my touch though the bodies
were not. The fur was cells telling themselves
to spin to keep her warm to stand
and hunt and keep. It was a red
autumn leaf on the forest floor, but
it was a blooded brown leaf, and another, because
they dragged the bodies to create a monument
to domination, to the enormous human,
and if I bore a child who suffered to see this,
or if I bore a child who gladdened to see this, or if
I bore a child who kept walking, I could not bear
it, so I will not bear one.

—Gretchen Primack

FIGHTERS

Braden stood at the edge of Jimmy's driveway and listened to the whimpering mutt drag her swollen belly down the gravel until the thin wire around her neck lashed into its scar, that ring of hard skin beneath her fur, solid as bone.

Jimmy yelled at Braden. "You looking at my bitch?"

"Huh?"

"My bitch. That's what they're called."

Jimmy's bitch moaned, a noise like falling rocks. The sound choked Braden's mind like a collar.

"My dad kicks her," Jimmy said. "I tell him when he kicks my bitch now, he's kicking all her pups, but he kicks her anyway."

"Watcha gonna do with her pups?"

"I dunno."

Braden waited until his own father's pickup sped off, then found his mom still in bed, cutting pictures from *Self* magazine. "Can we keep Jimmy's bitch's pups? They'll die if we don't."

His mother's feet dangled over the covers, long, yellow toenails like fangs. She never wore socks. She coughed, said,

"That bitch is a fighter. Saddest part of fighters is they live through everything." She looked at Braden. "Then they give birth to more fighters. Don't you worry about them pups. They'll live."

—APRIL RANGER

YOUR MOTHER SAYS, "I'M JUST SUPRISED YOU'RE NOT ANGRIER AT HIM, THAT'S ALL"

i. The dog bites you. The men come to take it away,
and the women in the clean white dresses coddle you
like a newborn child—they wipe away the blood
and tell you how much worse it could have been,
and how you deserved none of it. The neighbors say
they saw it coming, like that's supposed to make you
feel better. It wasn't the surprise that hurt you.
It was the teeth.

ii. When I am eight, I start going to a new school.
I learn just how high I can go on the swings with no one
to push me. After a few months, three girls tell me
they'll be my friends, "but only on Tuesdays and Thursdays."
I can't remember ever having felt so grateful.

iii. You came home one day, and the dog was waiting
for you on the porch like it had come home, too.
You let it in, and since then you've been its girl.
You picked the burs from its fur and it licked
the wounds you couldn't quite reach, and almost
every night, you slept in the same bed. It hated collars,
but sometimes it would wear one for you,
and what is that if not love?

iv. Before I become a lonely woman, I am an angry child.
One day I break every plate in the cupboard, and then
I sob for hours. It is easier to hate myself
when I give myself reasons to. I would rather blame
this body, the one thing that will never leave me for long.

v. They ask you if the dog has a history
of violence, and you say "no," and you mean it.
History is more than just the end—the dog with its bloody
jaws and you with your pain, your ugly, wailing scream
that echoes so loud the whole neighborhood can hear it.
It is the warm bed. It is the licked wounds. It is the coming
home. It is the collar, the one you forced around its neck
and told yourself it would grow to love. It is the part of you
that will always be its girl, even if it was never your dog.

vi. I kiss him first, and if there is fault to be found
here, doesn't this make it mine? I kiss him first.
It is easier to hate myself when I give myself reasons to.

vii. When a dog bites a person, or another dog,
the men come to take it away and the dog is put down.
They look at you strangely when you ask for the body.
They don't understand why you want a thing that has hurt you.
When the doctors are done with you, when their concern
and good intentions have stopped dulling the pain,
you leave the hospital with nothing to bury.

—JAZ SUFI

HOLE IN IT

After the dog has to be put to sleep,
you can feel the hole when you walk
into the library by the mural of baby
Achilles being dipped into the numbing
river but also when you walk into the forest.
Everything has a hole in it, not just Monday
or cut roses on the third day or Sears,
everything is a tornado with a pupil so
the tears can get out and the dreams
which is why you keep having to buy wine
glasses your friends keep breaking doing
their good deed of trying to clean up
and it's as if you haven't seen them
for years, you're an echo in a well
and the dog's still looking for you like
you're toy because of the hole in your chest
like the bottom of a flowerpot, sadness
sticking out like fuzz off a dandelion,
the filaments waving like kelp around
a deep-sea rift, a hole like the center
of the universe, a long tube of the dimensions
in knots like flight paths around Chicago
or Mozart. Sometimes the holes make breath
into music even if the lips try to stop it
something simple still gets through like
air or melody or love, like a pipe
in a mansion, a breeze through the bulwarks,
a throat connecting mouth to lungs and
intestines like a wick only hollow but
that's still where the flames attach.

—DEAN YOUNG

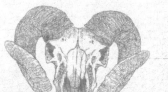

THE ANIMAL
IN ME
WANTS TO SEE
THE ANIMAL
IN YOU

*The creatures outside looked from pig to man,
and from man to pig, and from pig to man again;
but already it was impossible to say which was which*
—George Orwell

THE GHOST OF THE AUTHOR'S MOTHER HAS A CONVERSATION WITH HIS FIANCÉE ABOUT HIGHWAYS

...and down south, honey. When the side of the road began to swell with dead and dying things, that's when us black children knew it was summer. Daddy didn't keep clocks in the house. Ain't no use when the sky round those parts always had some flames runnin' to horizon, lookin' like the sun was always out. Back when I was a little girl, I swear, them white folk down south would do anything to stop another dark thing from touching the land, even the nighttime. We ain't have streetlights, or some grandmotherly voice riding through the fields on horseback tellin' us when to come inside. What we had was the stomach of a deer, split open on Route 59. What we had was flies resting on the exposed insides of animals with their tongues touching the pavement. What we had was the smell of gunpowder and the promise of more to come, and, child, that'll get you home before the old folks would break out the moonshine and celebrate another day they didn't have to pull the body of someone they loved from the river. I say "river" because I want you to always be able to look at the trees without crying. When we moved east, I learned how a night sky can cup a black girl in its hands and ask for forgiveness. My daddy sold the pistol he kept in the sock drawer and took me to the park. Those days, I used to ask him what he feared, and he always said "the bottom of a good glass." And then he stopped answering. And then he stopped coming home altogether.

Something about the first day of a season, child. Something always gotta sacrifice its blood. Everything that has its time must be lifted from the earth. My boys don't bother with seasons anymore. My sons went to sleep in the spring once and woke up to a motherless summer. All they know now is that it always be colder than it should. I wish I could fix this for you. I'm sorry none of my children wear suits anymore. I wish ties didn't remind my boys of shovels, and dirt, and an empty living room. They all used to look so nice in ties. I'm sorry that you may come home one day to the smell of rotting meat, the smell of a gutted thing left out to cook in a blazing heat, every calendar you own torn off the walls, burning in a trashcan.

And it will be the end of spring.
And you will know.

—HANIF WILLIS-ABDURRAQIB

MOSQUE IN GALILEE

Sketching the outlines of the country
I know by heart now how far I travel
From Haifa to the sea of Galillee

We passed a ruined mosque on the road
Not knowing if it was destroyed in '48 or '67 or '73
One wall buckling, a corner of the room lying open to the fields

The mihrab blackened by fire
Still marking the qibla for absent worshipers
Across the street a dead cow lying on its side

Three ropes hang down from the minaret
Some Hasidic boys have scaled up the side and sit
on the balcony eating sandwiches saying their prayers

What are they listening to? Is it the language of the land,
or the abandoned mosque, or is it that limp carcass
on the side of the road—

—Kazim Ali

AUBADE FOR ONE STILL UNCERTAIN OF BEING BORN

Lie still. Make their desperate hunt for your heart
beat them frenzied and let them second-guess
your muted tempo as counterfeit for their own.
Press your palm, still learning to unfurl,
to your den's wet beams and steady yourself
against the doorjamb of your lair; it will be time
when it is time. If your mother is a horse—and I am,
I am—let her approach Troy with you still hidden
within. Let her carry you like a bouquet of splinters
in her belly of timber still hot from hatching
at the future for firewood like it was a family tree.
All your life they will surround you, will stalk and strain
to hear that ballad from your canary pipes, will tempt
your quiet cover, will kick the keg of your desire
until it is dented nameless; all your life they will try
to say you are built for something else. It begins now—
so hush, hush: be nothing, just this once.

—Meg Day

ELEGY FOR AN ELECTROCUTED ELEPHANT

Bury the elephant
    where it fell, bone down
in the needle bed dirt—

that end-of-century husbandry
    whose marriage to electricity
was short lived.

Irony that separates us
    from the animals, and rapture
which holds its breath

until we're gone: the animal in me
    wants to see
the animal in you

go down on one knee,
    like the elephant Edison executed
on film in 1903.

Dust and dumbshow:
    love's gray degradations.
The elephant deserved to die,

but only the executioner knows why—
    and you and I,
who flipped the switch

and did not look away
    when the animal stiffened
and keeled and fell to its side,

but planted lilies there
      to trumpet our bereavement
and overtake the hide.

What have I come to kill
      or praise
that isn't already buried

by its imperfections,
      out of which
flowers grow?

—ROBIN EKISS

from I WRITE TO YOU FROM THE SEA

There are things still to be saved.

The waves trip over themselves
and are largely unhurt.

The trick's to keep building
themselves of themselves.

     If you were here,

you'd say I shouldn't worry the water,
or make overmuch
of my hereness as I'm so inclined.

Slumped against the white of my boat,

I invite the sea to make
a thing of me.

Out here I am garish

as a pit, a red sequined scarf
let slip to the floor.

It isn't decent, the way a scarf
can forget so quick
the neck shape it belonged to.

One reveal of skin
could slice wide a room and inside

the room there'd be desire,
red and sort of smooshed.

A deer open on the road.
An open deer on the memory

of a road. The sudden white
of the open neckline is suddenly
dishonest.

When a girl

with her overwhite skin agitates
a small enclosure like a room,

she makes of herself a wave. Then
she makes a pearl.

You are irritated
by my bringing up the girl.

She doesn't belong. She'll make
something hard of the story.

She'll make something hard
and round inside the story

—LAURA EVE ENGEL

MOOSE

Moose are drawn to roadsides during rain,
explains Olga over breakfast at an artist colony in Vermont.
Sporting wide-rimmed bifocals—eyes dulled from reading
by kerosene light—she wears her dark hair parted in the middle,
pulled back tight in a bun, and her shirt sleeves rolled
up her arms. Again I find myself in the company of women.
The others are matronly, mostly mothers and grandmothers
from Midwestern states, and a Mormon college girl from Idaho,
all poets, oatmeal-replenished. Her friend Amanda once hit a moose,
Olga continues, on a miserable morning, such as today, in Minnesota.
The animal bolted out of the hazy greenery as if expulsed from the kingdom
of ancient trees. She veered but time and space collided and she hit the beast,
her truck pounded into crushed metal, hissing steam mingling with
the drizzle. The moose vanished into the quivering spring thicket.
Shaken but unharmed, Amanda called for help. Olga and three other
women arrived, they searched at length, locating the young male dead.
They dragged, then tied the stag onto the pick-up and drove
home. I imagine Olga in charge, draining the buck's blood,
scooping out the viscera, the heart, her fingers between pancreas
and liver, her crawling inside the herbivore, hacking at the flesh,
dividing the venison five ways. I think: I will write a poem
about this and Elizabeth Bishop would not be happy,
but like the moose, she is dead. When I look at Olga I see
her snip the scrotum with her knife, letting the sac dangle
between her teeth. What did it taste like? the girl asks.
Meat, Olga shrugs, it tasted like pure meat.

—JOSEPH LEGASPI

DEER

They hang her in the barn, head down, tongue fat,
dripping blood. I am left alone
for a moment, venture close to stroke dark fur
made rough by winter; that is when she is still
whole, intact, before butchering. I'm not sure
if they shot her or hit her by accident
with the truck, but she comes from the mountains
out of season so it is the darkness that counts, not
how she died. All winter long we'll eat her
in secret: steaks, stews, bones boiled for broth
and the dogs. But what I will remember are men's hands—
fingers stained with oil and blood—
the rough way they turn back the hide, jerk down hard
to tear it off her body. A dull hunting
knife cracks and disjoints the carcass.
Dismembers it piece by piece.
The hide disappears—left untanned, buried,
taken to the dump. For years afterward
I walk out to the barn, scrape my foot against
the stained floor beneath the crossbeam, never tell anyone
                I've been taken like that:
without thanks, without a prayer, by hands
that didn't touch me the way a gift should be touched,
knives that slid beneath my skin out of season
and found only flesh, only blood.

—DEBORAH A. MIRANDA

TANNING PROCESS

Gardens are no longer wonders,
but fingernails to be trimmed.
And Koi ponds, once swimming
with flash and omens,
are all flat brass coins.

What about the gods?

The dumb, beast-headed, castrated,
wild, terracotta, snake-spined gods.

None too smart.
Years of enlightenment
ahead of them.

A stag charges a suburban, plate-glass sliding door,
in stark refusal to believe this house exists beneath
the limbs of ash trees at dusk.
Disbelief in blood and blinking glass.
Antlers tangled in oak floorboards.

The family hugs their sheets close,
grabs at
aluminum baseball bats,
counts their earrings,
reassures
that each bangle is in its place.

None too smart.
But the gods?
They have long lives,

long enough to stomp houses flat,
tear apart family portraits, glass coffee tables,
diplomas and ceiling fans
with blood-tipped horns.

Long enough to learn
to exit eagerly
through the shattered door, shake off
their lacerated hide
and walk the evening
in the skin of a man.

—CHRISTIAN REES

JUXTAPOSING THE ROAD KILL & MY BODY

The difference is the deer, somewhere
between severed & smashed, did not limp
back to his quiet home

      The difference is the boy was not a car

The difference is I saw it coming, slowly

      The difference is I was told thank you after

The difference is half of a deer,
blood emptied & insides
fashioned into a skirt,
is still called a deer

      A man, emptied of his voice
      & drawers ruined & sweet with grenadine,
      is called a myth or a bitch or not a man at all.

—DANEZ SMITH

EURYDICE

It's still dark here.
  My voice weaves
    through the cracks
of a halved piano.
  That sound a doe makes
    when the arrowhead
replaces the day
  with an answer to the rib's
    hollowed hum.
We saw it coming
  but kept walking through the hole
    in the garden. Because the leaves
were pure green & the fire
  only a pink brushstroke
    in the distance. It's not
about the light—but how dark
  it makes you depending
    on where you stand.
Depending on where you stand
  your name can sound like a full moon
    shredded in a dead doe's pelt.
Your name changed when touched
  by gravity. Gravity breaking
    our kneecaps just to show us
the sky. Why did we keep saying Yes—
  even with all those birds.
    Who would believe us
now? My voice cracking
  like bones inside the radio.
    Silly me. I thought love was real

& the body imaginary.
  I thought a little chord
    was all it took. But here we are—
standing in the cold field
  again. Him calling for the girl.
    The girl beside him.
Frosted grass
  snapping
    beneath her hooves.

—Ocean Vuong

UNTIL THE MAGGOT IS KING OVER BODY

WHY ALL OUR LITERARY PURSUITS ARE USELESS
Eighty-five percent of all existing species are beetles and various forms
of insects. English is spoken by only 5 percent of the world's population.

WHY THERE MAY BE HOPE
One of the greatest stories ever written is the story of a man who
wakes to find himself transformed into a giant beetle.
                                                    —Mary Ruefle

THE EARTHQUAKE SHE SLEPT THROUGH

                              She slept through the earthquake in Spain.
The day after was full of dead things. Well, not full but a few.
Coming in the front door, she felt the crunch of a carapace

under her foot. In the bathroom, a large cockroach
rested on its back at the edge of the marble surround; the dead
antennae announced the future by pointing to the silver mouth

that would later gulp the water she washed her face with.
Who wouldn't have wished for the quick return
of last night's sleep? The idea, she knew, was to remain awake,

and while walking through the day's gray fog, trick the vaporous
into acting like something concrete: a wisp of cigarette smoke,
for instance, could become a one-inch Lego building

seen in the window of a bus blocking the street.
People sometimes think of themselves as a picture that matches
an invented longing: a toy forest, a defaced cricket, the more

or less precious lotus. The night before the quake, she took a train
to see a comic opera with an unlikely plot. She noticed a man
in a tan coat and necktie who looked a lot like Kafka.

The day after, she called a friend to complain about the bugs.
From a distant city—his voice low and slightly plaintive—he said,
Are you not well? Is there anything you want?

—MARY JO BANG

METAMORPHOSIS

Eat the egg
shell while
you have
a mouth:
in ten days,
little instar,
you will die
without it

—Malachi Black

AUBADE IN WHICH THE BATS TRIED TO WARN ME

You used to recite the parts of my body like psalms.
    I should have known when you started to kiss
        with your eyes closed that your mouth would ruin us.

And I should have known when you slipped belladonna
    in my buttonholes, when you started to bring me empty boxes,
        when I found her dog asleep under our house.

She told me about someone she'd been sleeping with,
    and the someone was you. At first, I didn't tell you I knew.
        I came home, and you were slicing rhubarb and strawberries.

You put sugared hands on my neck and kissed my forehead.
    No, it happened like this. When you fucked me, I could feel
        how much you hated me. And you came. And I came twice.

You stayed on top and softened inside me as you kissed
    my shoulders. I stayed awake to watch you sleep and thought
        about the stories your parents told about you. The wildfire

you started. How you broke your mother's birdhouses.
    How your father paid you to kill bats, a dollar a body.
        Last summer you let me watch. As you waited with a racket,

timber wolves announced the moon, bats crept out of the attic.
    The soft pulp of their bodies struck the house. Your father swatted
        your back, handed you five bucks, and I went to pick up the bats.

One still shuddered against the cinderblock. I should have left,
    but I didn't. I crushed its head with a rock and tossed it into the woods
        and went inside and washed my hands and lied to you.

—Traci Brimhall

BETTER THAN THE PROFESSIONALS

My mother has become an amateur exterminator,
better than the professionals. A self-taught cockroach assassin.
Maybe you have one in the family, too. She can crush roaches
with a roll of paper, the bottom of a shoe, a slipper.
But no matter how hard I try, she says, our home can never be
beautiful because of these zang lang. She slams a drawer precisely
shut as they crawl up to the edge. She flattens them
with chopsticks, skewers them with forks. Once, I wake to her
silent figure, right above me, a sword of newspaper in her hand,
a slime of insect across a headline. All that night, I feel my hair
for tiny legs. But maybe, like me, eventually you learn
the art—fear swallowed, you cut off escape routes with a well-
placed French textbook so your mother can swoop in
for a masterful coup de grâce. Or perhaps you have performed
solo, have stood alone afterwards at the kitchen sink
to wash away the sticky remains, to purge yourself,
though the notices posted around the apartment complex all point
their official fingers at you, you for snacking in the living room
& in your own room with friends, for leaving out a bowl
of half-finished breakfast the morning you're late for the bus.
& the fingers point to your mother, too tired to clean it all
immediately, too fed up to get up again, another morning
in the same dirty apartment. The clean, official fingers
point & your mother goes back to sleep, dreams of holding
a blowtorch, fueled by her own screaming heart. Yes,
she dreams of burning the apartment down, her voice
flaming into the flaming air, *The landlord doesn't know shit!*

—CHEN CHEN

113

MY HEART KICKED LIKE A MOUSE IN A PAPER BAG

I was on the cleaning crew for two dollars an hour,
wheeling a trash cart through the aisles at Sears,
panning for cigarettes in the sand of ashtrays, fumbling
fluorescent tubes that exploded when they hit the floor.
I once removed the perfect turd from a urinal, fastidiously
as an Egyptologist handling the scat of a pharaoh.

Some of the janitor's boys were black men with white hair;
the rest wore badges with missing letters in Spanish.
We heard four bells and galloped across the store.
The janitor sat all day in the boiler room
reading Asian mail-order bride magazines.

I was the boy who swam in trash. I dumped the carts
into the compacter we dubbed the Crusher, then
leaped on the pile to pack it down. Sometimes,
I'd jump on the garbage and burst through
like a skater too heavy for the ice on a frozen lake.
Once a trashman who did not see me pressed the button,
and the walls of the Crusher began to grind. I yelled
and the grinding stopped. The janitor never knew;
he was masturbating in the boiler room.

A stock boy handed me a paper bag one night
as if it were the lunch he forgot to eat, and punched out.
The bag was alive. There was a mouse inside, kicking,
caught sniffing around the Crusher. Bewildered boy
that I was, I called security, department store cops
who loitered at the loading dock, breath hot
from smoking, hunting shoplifters and telling lies
about the war. One of them said: *Where's the mouse?*

When he clapped the bag in his hands it popped, and the pop
made me flinch, and the flinch made him slam the bag again,
till the strawberry stain told me the interrogation was over.
He flipped the bleeding sack at me, and walked away.
My heart kicked like a mouse in a paper bag.

Today I stomp on the trash behind the shed, packing it down for the barrels
I steer into the road. Gathering the cigarettes I do not smoke, that float
in the coffee I do not drink, satisfies the cleaning crew in me.
I hear the four bells like a fighter with the same headache for forty years.
Sometimes I search the garbage with a flashlight for an unpaid bill,
a bottle of pills, a lost letter, the perfect mouse to liberate.

—MARTÍN ESPADA

AUBADE ENDING WITH THE DEATH OF A MOSQUITO

—at Apollo Hospital, Dhaka

Let me break

        free of these lace-frail
        lilac fingers disrobing

the black sky

        from the windows of this
        room I sit helpless, waiting

silent—sister,

        once you drew from me
        the coil of red twine loneliness

spools inside—

        once, I wanted to say one
        true thing. As in, *I want more*

from this life,

        or, *the sky is hurt, a blue vessel.*
        We pass through each other

like weary

        sweepers haunting through glass
        doors, arcing across gray floors

faint trails

        of dust we leave behind—he
        touches my hand, waits for me

to clutch

        back. From this cold marble
        floor, mosquitoes rise like smoke

from altars,

        seeking the blood still
        humming our unsaved bodies.

I make a fist

        around this one leaving raised
        raw kisses on our bare necks—

once I woke

        to the myth of one life, willed
        myself into another—how strange

to witness,

        Sister, the nameless shape our
        mingled blood impresses across

my open palm.

—TARFIA FAIZULLAH

SOMETHING ABOUT JOY

Can't say it comes naturally—the spring
and seltzer that swing the shoulders—
for mine is a stiff-necked people, more
at home in a home surrounded by dark
than daylight. Trust not the sun, sister.
The moon at least is earnestly obscure.
Something about joy is liquid, quicksilver
and giddy on fumes, but my blood
is a Soviet Bloc. I find the word "toil"
very appealing, like truncated turmoil
or treacherous soil spilling its pathos
into an honest day's work. Something
about joy resists even this poem; I catch
flashes of it, a peripheral rabbit, and tell
myself that even if I brought it home
the cat would just eat it. The cat would
sit by the screen with a shit-eating grin
and groom herself with a mouth full
of my joy, souring. Then again, I love
the cat, and something about joy says
leave the good stuff out, even if
your friends are drunk already—they
dance so beautifully, your friends.

—DINAH FAY

BUT FIRST

There is a holiness to exhaustion
is what I keep telling myself, filling out

forms to get my TA paid, making copies
on the hot and heaving machine, writing

Strong start on a pretty bad poem. And then
it's the children: the baby's mouth

open, going for the breast, the girl's hair
to wash tonight and then comb so

painstakingly in the tub while the conditioner
drips onto her shoulders, while her

discipline chart at school flaps in the air
conditioner, taped on a filing cabinet, longing

for stickers. My heart is so giant tonight,
like one of those moons so full

and beautiful and terrifying if you see it
while you're getting out of the car

you have to go inside the house
and make someone else come out

and see it for themselves. I want
everything, I have to admit. I want *yes*

and I want it all the time. I want a clean

heart. I want the children to sleep

and the drought to end. I want the rain
to come down—*It's supposed to monsoon*

is what Naomi said, driving off
this morning, and she was right as usual.

It's monsooning. And still I want, even
as the streets are washed clean

and then begin to flood, even though the man
came again today to check the rat traps

and said he bet we'd catch the rat within twenty-four hours.
We still haven't caught the rat so I'm working

at the table with my legs folded up beneath me.
I want to know what is holy—I do. But first

I want the rat to die. I am thirsty for that death
and will drink deeply of that victory, the twack

of the trap's horrible toothed jaw, and I will rush
to see the evidence—no matter how gruesome, I will

rush to lean over and peer behind the washing
machine. You see? That's exactly what I mean.

—CARRIE FOUNTAIN

PROMENADE À DEUX

We began by two-stepping barefoot
in the kitchen. I looked into his face like a farmer
looks into a horse's mouth, trying to conjure
the future from the now. His hands
were two small animals beneath my blouse, soft
and frantic. Long ago the clouds
in their white gowns still rode their white mares
sidesaddle across the manageable sky
snd everyone I loved was incidentally
still alive. When I was eight, I put my last quarter
in a gumball machine at the video rental place
and no gumball came out. I can't say I grieved
the quarter, exactly, but the distance I saw
chasming between the beginning and the end
of a desire. That night, as he was leaving,
he touched my braid like it was something that hurt me.
I can't stand the way men touch
gently after knowing they've wounded you.

This morning I woke up to two scorpions that,
while mating, had fucked themselves
right into a glue trap. Still, they went at it.
Wikipedia says a scorpion can live for up to twelve months
without food or water. I watched them as I drank
my coffee, as I sliced and ate a peach. So, this is loneliness:
Two scorpions fucking each other to death in a glue trap
and no one to share it with.

—MEG FREITAG

DOMESTIC BUILDUP

There is a way sleep can leave a person
and there is a way sleep can leave a whole house.
You are the one with the darker skin, the ordered
and well-built mind and I am the one who wakes
and cries in the night. Often we drive home late
and lay with our limbs untouching until dawn.
The night you find the rat, cornered at the floorboards
and searching for water, you say to me: How
do I end it.

—Blake Lee Pate

ODE TO THE WHITE-LINE-SWALLOWING HORIZON

Apologies to the moths
that died in service to my
windshield's cross-country journey.
Apologies to the fine country
cooking vomited into a rest stop bathroom.
Apologies to the rest stop janitor.
To the mop, galvanized bucket,
sawdust, and push broom—the felled
tree it was cut from, dulled saw, blistered hand,

I offer my apologies. To the road.
To the white-line-swallowing horizon.
I've used you almost up.

I'm sorry I don't know another way
to push the charcoal outline of that house
into the ocean-dark behind me.
For being a grown man
with a boogeyman at his back.
Apologies to the grown man growing out
of a splintering boy's body.
Apologies to the splinters. Little ones,
you should've been a part of something whole.

—Jamaal May

BLACK WITCH MOTH

The moth lifts its dress and everything beneath
the hem's shadow sings—the grasses where lie
the dead bull and flies skating across its still-
open eyes, its mouth crusted over with clover
and spit while the maggots swim their
patient circuits where the bull's genitals
have rotted and dropped their bells. The moth
slips through gnat-swarmed air onto the bull's hooves
and flies past the bull's corpse, beyond the outskirts
of the barnyard. No dust from the moth's pleats—
opening and closing—drops onto the dead
animal's choir. A boy sees its black dress bob
above him, sees in its shadow an angel to call his own.
Let a sudden finish overcome him wherever
the wild shadow lies flat its news, lies motionless
its wingdom among the barnyard grass.
Let the earth take in the boy as it will the bull.
And the worm-work done unto him as unto the bull.
His color gone and bone given into an end
making permanent the final pose of his suffering,
crux into crux his body returning into itself
as though into the first cell that split
until skin, until marrow, until heart, until the maggot
is king over body. Let the boy's skin be a tearing,
to see it torn from him and wonder how
then wonder how far until the next time, the next boy.
The moth flashes open its dress then not,
flash then not, flaps over the dead boy, its shadow
moving up his thigh to the hip, to the torso,

lifting its garment across his nakedness.
And the bull into the earth. And the boy into the earth.
And the earth not full, the earth not full.

—PHILLIP B. WILLIAMS

IN WHAT MANNER WE WILL JOIN THEM

Animal myths, like that of a human consumed by a wolf, depend upon a girl
—Bhanu Kapil

Whole years will be spent, underneath these impossible stars, / when dirt's the only animal who will sleep with you / & touch you with / its mouth.
—Aracelis Girmay

FAR NORTH

I was born from the body of a rattlesnake cloven
by a rusty shovel. This was in Jackson, a prison town.
Signs along the highway read DO NOT
PICK UP HITCHHIKERS. Its spasming halves.
The after-rattle. I was born in a back yard
pocketed with shrubs in which furred beasts
hid wet fangs, before the edge of woods
in which hovered the filtered dim
of a shallow sea. I was four years old.
When I say I was born from my father's hands
gripping the shovel, his strength thrust in the dirt,
I mean that before this snake shook its dice
in its can, its tongue near enough to lick my shin,
I had no memory or mind. My father was young
and the blade bit deep and the snake's two lengths
shook a good while. I was born then
in my father's shadow as the snake's tepid blood
dribbled in the dirt and its smooth muscle
coiled and cooled, two partners in a dance,
as if one mind still spoke through both.
I have seen children born. The cruelty
and guts of it. The spill and wail.
I watched the living sleeve go limp
and knew it could have filled with me,
sucked me through its teeth. I was a wick
from which a bell had lifted.
I flickered into focus. I was four years old
in Jackson, a factory town hundreds of miles
too far north for rattlers. No one
told me this story. My father denies
both snake and shovel. No one remembers but me:

sun dimming through leaves, twilight air
growing chill, the woods' dark gathering
to pour toward us. I took my first breath.
I did. Or I'd have never made it
to the house before the black wave broke.

—Scott Beal

THIS MORNING I READ THE WIKIPEDIA ARTICLE FOR "HUMAN"

The tone is detached and formal. I am sitting in bed and the way my fingers click against this keyboard. I tab over. Pornhub.com/gay. Tab. Vintage. Tab. How I feel watching a bareback video from the early '80s is how I feel watching the MGM lions roar. I don't care. I just want to see an open mouth. I just want to see an opening.

—EMILY BROWN

WANT

abandoned by his coyote, my
father, sand seething beneath
his sneakers,   trekked
through   southern Arizona:
maze of acacia   & cholla
cold sweat cut   his face like
a razor   in his pocket: a fine-
tooth comb,   dice, & a photo
of a girl playing a violin   on
the third day,   he picked up
a rock,   killed a blue lizard
with a single strike   he tore it
apart,   shoved guts & bones
into his mouth   the first
time I knelt for a man,   my
lips   pressed to his zipper,
I suffered   such hunger

—Eduardo Corral

DREAM WITH AN EMPTY CHAMBER

Before I return to that ruinous city of lonely
smoke stacks, puffing rotten clouds against
graysky, I catch you inside another woman,
your coyote's coat strewn on the floor, body of
a hungry man, wrong in every beautiful wrong
way. I pull the revolver from my coat. Fire.
Casings evaporate before they hit the floor.
I want to see what shred bullets can do to
flesh, how they pierce and lodge hard in the bone.

                              I am standing at your hollow
door, turning the key. There are too-wet towels littering the hall
from the bathroom to the bedroom. I haven't seen her face.
Surrender your hands as your mouth bleats. Tell me it's not
what I thought. Not the confession you transmit from towers. Go
ahead. Time it to the cylinder's *click click click click*.

In the morning, everything burns. Hairs inside my nose, curled
            and brittle darlings. Throat, after-clawed. Hands sweat-
fresh and black with residue. A finch jangles a chime outside
            my window. This bed will never know the rattle of pelvis
against wrist, my begging grip, what giving up looks
            like, though I know I've already pulled the trigger.
                        Buried the gun in the snow.

—Aricka Foreman

CARCASS

In the car, they are a gleam of sweat, a hotbox of mercy.
He rides her as a fang into the nape. The moon, a careful
witness, makes open the excuse for the indulge. It is vacant,
this kind of animal. It is blood, this kind of thirst. "Sex
is for the dead", he says and she is a clawless night.
"Your black is forbidden", he says and she is a good
time. "What is your name?", he asks and she is nowhere
to be found.

—Tonya Ingram

ODE TO MY CAT EUCLID

Mackerel sky above my dinner bell,
A chicken flies across the sun.
A tail floats around a corner in smoothest luxury.
Loving fool, you are no serf among my kingdom.
Piano keys breathe onto your lamp
As gravity wraps its vectors around your bones.
In the next life I see you batting
At the noon-toiled flies in your eyes.
For now its jazz can up swat down woo-wee,
Just glinting like a moon-child,
Scooting like a scooter should.

—Noelle Kocot

SELF-PORTRAIT, WEARING BEAR SKULL AS MASK

The world looks like fangs.
You look like fangs to the world.
Everything is quieter
so you shout, slang and other language
coming out warbled and hungry
as a barbed arrow.
The world does not care what you eat
so long as it is not them,
but motherfuck, they all look ripe
from the inside of a mouth.
The mouth is a cave and you are the fire
within, or you are the cave painting,
the ghost of something slain by something larger,
or the mouth is the scope of a rifle
and you are a boy away from home.
You are a boy in the shape of animal
and in the dark everything feels like the woods.
The sweat, the fresh smack of spring
brings blood to your face
but you are still just skull and imagined claw
to the world, just the dumb perfect body
of death. You stopped speaking long ago.
You haven't eaten yet today,
and the world looks bright as winter.

—MICHAEL MLEKODAY

LITTLE DEAD WOLVES

Fed up, I take a kitchen knife to my belly. It would be dramatic to say it is the only smile my body has made in months but it is the only smile my body has made in months. & then the little dead wolves. They gush, sparrow-sized, from the wound. Their fur glitters with blood & fat. It is endless. Little dead wolves & little dead wolves. I sit in a kitchen chair & watch as they tumble onto the floor, as they slide up against the dishwasher on runnels of thick, dark fluid. Soon I am up to my waist in little dead wolves & it is not stopping. I pull myself to the top of them but still they spill & spill. Days go by & they burst through the windows. The house crumples under the weight of them. Now I am in a field of little dead wolves. Finally, after a time, it is over. I sew myself up with wolf bones & wolf hair. & then I begin to build. A mansion of little dead wolves with little dead wolf furniture: little dead wolf end tables & little dead wolf armoires & little dead wolf chandeliers & around the house I build a wall of little dead wolves & around the wall I build a moat of little dead wolves & around the moat I build a forest of little dead wolves & you never touched me again.

—Jeremy Radin

HAUNTED
For Bucky

We are looking for you everywhere.
Trying to find a path
between drooping trees.
Listening for your rustle
under bamboo,
brush of fig leaves,
feeling your leap
onto the porch.
We see your raised face
at both sides of a day.
How was it, you lived around
the edge of everything we did,
seasons of ailing & growing,
mountains of laundry & mail?
I am looking for you first & last
in the dark places,
when I turn my face away
from headlines at dawn,
dropping the rolled news to the floor.
Your rumble of calm
poured into me.
There was the saving grace
of care, from day one, the watching
and being watched
from every corner of the yard.

—NAOMI SHIHAB NYE

LADY, THAT'S A LEMUR GET OUT OF MY CROTCH

was exactly what I thought, after
the woman tried to engage
in that particular kind of endearing conversation
between my legs. It was quite uncomfortable
how she smiled after noticing
the sticker of a "cute cat" on my phone case, which
wasn't a cat at all. Instead of telling her
it was a lemur, or crying, or telling her
to stop the whole thing, I looked up at the cracked,
graveyard ceiling of the Planned Parenthood
& imagined all of the eyes that could've been looking
at me one day. One attempts to be significant like this
in moments when you finally feel
the control that you should've had all along.
It feels slimy & foreign but just when you think you could
get used to it, the woman, who could have been anybody, smiles
& incorrectly identifies the mammal on your phone case.
She could have been anybody, & she could have been smart.
Maybe it was the stench of death that confused her into
thinking things weren't actually what they were. She can be
forgiven for this, obviously.
What does this have to do with lemurs?
Mostly everything
because they were there, that complete dying species, in the room
where I half was. They were doing lemur-like things,
as lemurs often do, disappearing in & out of existence.
They should have been in Madagascar where there's
a tree forming a new ring that I am, somehow, a part of.
If they were smart they'd be in Madagascar dying.
The lady hadn't looked up for a while now, it could have been
years. Could she tell how many things have died inside me?

That'd be awkward, like when your fly's unzipped & the whole
fifth grade knows about it, except you. & just like the fifth grade,
it was over. The lady squeezed my arm & left the room, leaving
me amongst the lemurs & half-deaths.
What we didn't know was how dumb it is to kill something
that was already dead in the first place.

—MARY ALICE STEWART

PITCH FOR A MOVIE: DINOSAURS IN THE HOOD

Let's make a movie called Dinosaurs In The Hood.
Jurassic Park meets *Friday* meets *The Pursuit of Happiness*.
There should be a scene where a little black boy is playing
with a toy dinosaur on the bus, then looks out the window
& sees the T-Rex, because there has to be a T-Rex.

Don't let Tarantino direct this. In his version, the boy plays
with a gun, the metaphor: black boys toy with their own lives,
the foreshadow to his end, the spitting image of his father.
Fuck that, the kid has a plastic Raptor or a Triceratops
& this is his proof of magic or God or Santa. I want a scene

where a cop car gets pooped on by a pterodactyl, a scene
where the corner store turns into a battle ground.
Don't let the Wayans brothers in this movie. I don't want any racist shit
about Asian people or any overused Latino stereotype mess.
This movie is about a neighborhood of royal folks,

children of slaves & immigrants & addicts & exile, saving their town
from real ass dinosaurs. I don't want some cheesy, yet progressive
Hmong Sexy Hot Dude Hero with a funny, yet strong, commanding
Black Girl buddy-cop-film. This is not a vehicle for Will Smith
& Sofia Vergara. I want grandmas on the front porch taking out raptors

with guns they hid in walls & under mattresses. I want those little spitty,
screamy dinosaurs. want Cecily Tyson to make a speech, maybe two.
I want Viola Davis to save the city in the last scene with a black fist afro pick
through the last dinosaurs long, scaled, cold-blood neck. & this can't be
a black movie. This can't be a black movie. This movie can't be dismissed

because of its cast or its audience. This movie can't be metaphor
for black people & extinction. This movie can't be about race.
This movie can't be about black pain or cause black people pain.
This movie can't be about a long history of having a long history with hurt.
This movie can't be about race. Nobody can say nigga in this movie

who can't say it to my face in public. No chicken jokes in this movie.
No bullets in the heroes. & no one kills the black boy. & no one kills
the black boy. & no one kills the black boy. Besides, the only reason
I want to make this is for that first scene: the little black boy on the bus
with a toy dinosaur, his eyes wide & endless

                         his dreams possible, pulsing, & right there.

                                        —Danez Smith

IDAHO

All summer
it was on fire
I was as always
in California,
looking out my window,
discovering nothing,
then flying back
east far
above those forests
filled with black
smoke to feel
again that way
I will keep
failing to name.
O the same mistakes
O the mythical
different results.
It's true one day
I walked a ridge
saw a hawk
read three letters
by Keats, bought
some postcards
I will never send,
and in a blue
scrawl made
a list then fell
asleep holding
volume twelve
of the old
encyclopedia

some stranger
sent to fill
me with pictures
and information
about that land
where no president
has ever been born.
I woke wanting
so much to go
inside the mountain
they call
The Cabinet
to find
a few bats
and the daughter
of the chambers
drawing ibex
on the walls
so I can ask
her how soon
and in what manner
we will join them.

—MATTHEW ZAPRUDER

AFTER

I sat on his sofa, spine bent like an antelope
stripped by a Hummer's teeth.

It would be easy to say he ground my bones
to road kill, limbs splayed for show.

But this is the way I always sit. My spine
incongruent, a mountain road

I choose not to follow. I am under
a shaded tree one minute

close my eyes & open them to discover
I am back in his kitchen, a rotten

cavity of who I was that morning.

How could I be raped one night
wake up with stitches down my legs

        & still feel like a goddess?

Feel in awe for being birthed
something new before the reality

hits, quicksands me into sidewalk?
I wilt sideways this time, collect

in the nearest bathroom & examine
the country of my body.

In the mirror: my antlers, a crown
seamed with blood ivory. Gigantic & proud.

Tomorrow I will close my eyes & pray.
Tomorrow I will close my eyes

& not hear him sing.

—FATIMAH ASGHAR

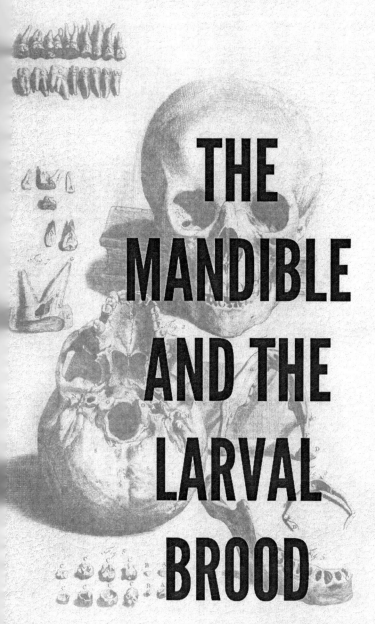

THE MANDIBLE AND THE LARVAL BROOD

...the relation between the human and nonhuman animal is constantly opened anew and, as it were, permanently. It is a wound, if you will, that can never be healed and is only further excavated and deepened by the very iterative technologies (thinking, writing, speech) that we use to try and suture it.
—Cary Wolfe

KINGS

Today I peel off the palm
of my hand. It burns
slow, a deep red, feels like
fighting and the sorrow
of a dying dog. The spring
creeps up like sticky vines
against solid oak, Sade
plays and thank god, the
high is deep and pulling,
it's this time of year where
all the dead animals come
to me, or leave themselves
to be found. Today I saw
the dog first, its belly
holding like a caldera, its
breath absent and only
just disappeared. The
cats lining the gutters
get covered with white
towels, their paws stuffed
with rose buds, I bike
past them, think about
eating the soft meat of
their thighs and bellies. My
mouth would look good
and frightening with the
tail hanging from my lips.
I don't remember
the month or the time of
year, but I remember
him

from the house down
the block, how he showed
me the scar on his hip,
asked me to touch it, did
you know that things
that start in our throats
can eventually travel
the whole body, sink
into the bone, viruses and
other misinformation.
The scar is eight inches
raised red, I follow the
straight line of it down his
hip, this is how the game
starts, it is just a game,
you know, just a child
playing with the king of
the neighborhood.

—Nic Alea

MOTHERHOOD: A SILK SCARF WITH HAND-PAINTED BLOOD HOUNDS

> *Sure, I wanted to believe violence was a little bell*
> *you could ring and get what you wanted*
> —*Carrie Fountain*

Every Sunday that summer, my mother dragged her darlings
to the heat of the brick and mortar pet store
to buy the bones of other beings for our sweetly dying dog.

There was certainty in the ritual. The plastic bag of marrow was always
four dollars, and it hung rhythmically from our mother's wrist
as we strolled across the parking lot, the little bell on the shop's door always

about to stop ringing behind us. But one Sunday, my mother spotted a baby
through the fogged window of a stranger's Buick, swaddled in a yellow blanket.
Alone. The hem was wrapped across its bitty mouth as if to say, Keep your hands

to yourself. There was a pay phone nearby. Our quarter clicked back
into its thoughtless head. Within an hour, our mother was a hero.
And yet. Why does it seem like every summer another news reporter

tells a similar story about a similar baby found in a suburban parking lot?
Each time it happens, I can't help but imagine a beautiful woman
dismissing motherhood with too much ease, shedding it

like a scarf with blood hounds vying through the silk, their teeth
falling away from her collarbone forever. That summer it was over
one hundred degrees at least once a week, and there was

light casting off of every pavement. I was still a girl. In the concrete I saw
silver. Like what a woman would cinch around her wrists while getting ready
for something special. I was still too young to know, but I asked

why. My mother would not tell me and the policeman would not tell me
and the pet store owner slipped behind the employee only door
with a dead canary, a yellow feather catching in her hangnail.

—LAUREN BERRY

NO ONE THINKS TOOLS ARE WHAT SEPARATES HUMANS FROM OTHER ANIMALS ANYMORE

This kind of thinking changed in the '60s. There has been much research and evidence since that time. Crows have been known to whittle and taper sticks to poke in holes. The people downtown use computers to make money. Wasps flatten mud by battering it with small stones. Dolphins use sea sponges to protect their noses when hunting on the ocean floor. In the SRO, room 301 uses a squeegee to make money to afford his room. Room 216 uses a bucket with a tight lid and shakes it hard to wash his laundry. Herons have been seen sprinkling food like breadcrumbs over the water to entice fish. Room 423 has Vicodin that she can sell in order to buy crack. Tech workers use their salaries to drive prices up. The suburban boy uses the internet to get information on where to buy a trenchcoat, on where to buy a ski mask, on where to buy a gun.

Orangutans make whistles from leaves to warn of predators. Room 339 goes from door to door late at night with his crack pipe, asking women if they want to buy the cigarettes he's stolen, if they want to smoke crack, if they want to suck his cock now that they've smoked his crack. Sea otters crack things open with shells. The suburban girl uses her tight tee shirt to get backstage at the Warfield. The suburban girl uses her tight tee shirt to get on the tour bus. The suburban girl uses her tight tee shirt to get in the hotel room. The suburban girl gets used. Sea otters crack things open with shells.

Macaques yank out human hair to use as dental floss. Parrots use pieces of metal or plastic to open their cages. Room 518 uses duct tape, uses pantyhose, uses Gillette, uses a wig and a knife to get home safely. In the department store, the professor uses his credit card to buy expensive lingerie for himself. Room 526 used a credit card to open the door of 423. Orangutans can pick a lock with a paperclip. The case manager for room 212 uses Wellbutrin and Klonopin; the tech worker uses Adderall and Ambien; room 411 uses rRsperidal and Ativan.

Capuchins make stone knives by banging flint against the floor. Wasps flatten mud by battering it with small stones. The man in room 205 used a hammer to kill the husband of the woman in 502. Now she uses crystals to keep evil away. She uses crystal to keep evil away. She pours sea salt on the floor, small white crystals. She takes a wrench because she doesn't have a hammer. She uses the wrench like a hammer. She uses the wrench to let the light into her head. She uses her head. It's a candle. It's a flashlight. It's a light bulb. It's a flash.

—DAPHNE GOTTLIEB

HOW TO MAKE A SHADOW

Give her the spirit of a dog,
a black dog with a sword in her paws. [1]
Tether her. Put Position
at the bottom of a well filled with rats;
rats with shining backs, their eyes shillings
in the pocket of a man who sweats,
sweats at the ass crack for Position.
Say to her, *bark* and she moans. Sudden chorus.
The grass sits up to listen and asks:
Who is the weed that will not sever?
Why won't the earth take water? Say, *bark*
and she bites the space between ankle and sole. Say, *no*,
to her. *Be quiet.* Like, may the seed stop up your throat.
Or, hold the sword between your teeth. Cut your tongue.
Say, *I nigger your heart, I eat your sleep.* I give you the dream
where you kneel and can't straighten.
Get down from here, into the well.
Fight the rat or let him ride like a disaster on your shoulders. Say, *no*.
Say, *don't open your mouth again.* Or try to open it
with a bridle there. I ride you when you're so small, small beast.
No.
It will ring as omen: smiling dead squirrel at the curb, shining scythe under a
bus bench,
dead birds in a nest, dark feather under the doormat.
Black tongue, black roof of mouth, black paw pads, black nails, black snout,
black spit.
Say, *die*, and she comes like a jinn,
silk shadow at your bedside:

---

1. From the vision at Messina, where a procession praying for help from the plague witnessed a
   "black dog with a drawn sword among them." *A Distant Mirror*, Barbara W. Tuchman.

I nigger your dreams,
bitter seed in the well of your throat. I will not scatter
from your heart. I grow a tree there.
I rest in its shadow.

—LADAN OSMAN

PETISM

Almost hitting an animal with your car might actually be scarier than hitting one. Like the time I slammed the brakes before a possum. It toppled over cleanly and rigid. It wasn't dead, just petrified. Just lying there in the way of my mom's Honda Odyssey. I have never seen so many dead animals as I did when I drove from Connecticut to Ohio. Shocked, then used to it, then shocked again when I considered the cumulative number at the end of the trip. I wasn't afraid. I am never afraid when something scary is happening. Only before or after. My sister and I got two puppies. Finally. My puppy ate rat poison. When I was younger the rats stayed outside in the garage and in the woodpile. You sew your own shroud. My puppy got too close to the river by the ranch and was eaten by a crocodile slash alligator. What animals? How many is shocking? I saw his face in a plain pine box. A plain white shroud and a plain pine box. It looked like a mask of skin. He was smiling. When I went home for Christmas a few rats ran under the couch. When I went home for Easter I sat on the couch and felt—Deadmaus—something still, fragile, bony. In the cushions of the couch was a mouse, petrified. You know, like those people who smile but without a soul. The funerals that I haven't been able to go to because I was further than a short plane ride away. Feeling the lack of seeing the tears of people I love. Christ has risen. God bless. There's a gasmask my boyfriend would love for me to make him wear. Lying alone in the sun in a Spanish concrete courtyard. I ate falafel and followed an ant with my eyes for many minutes. The ant stopped moving, stopped breathing. In death it is scary like that because it will never unfreeze, for me. They shake naturally like that but in the last moments—even before the heart actually stops, when induced—they go still. What about the animals that enjoy stillness? Is there something pleasing about a subtle death? If it were pleasing would it be alright? I loved my hamster. I gave it love through food. He died trapped in one of the tunnels in his home. He had a heart attack. He was obese. I am not okay with how often I can't keep or am made to be dead (not home) almost as what's most rewarded. I read a story about a woman who was prey of a crocodile.

—PUBBY

MENAGERIE

You, the unblinking, who stand for
the corporeal, are not real: I believe
in everything, but I do not believe
in your eyes, do not believe that I
am being seen by you, you who have gone
blind away into earth in spirit while here
your bones have been asked to continue
believing in one another, like an army
that has suddenly forgotten what it was
it was brought together to fight for.
Hence the little wires I know to be
woven through you like telephone lines
that make us believe we can still know
those we've abandoned, though I respect
the maker of eyes who made sure
to embed a sliver of silver or copper
in the glass, something to arrest us here,
to rivet us to this moment we are meant
to believe in, to believe that you, Bobcat,
are actually killing you, Field Mouse,
that you, Coyote, are actually howling,
and I am almost ready to believe in this
when I raise my heavy eyes up to the next tier
and see you, Vulture, perched as always
attendant above these deaths.

But then I realize that you are also dead
and as little conscious of death as the rest,
you whose purpose always seemed to be
to know death has occurred, and now here
you are, cotton-headed and cold in the thread-

bare shawl of your feathers, your glass eyes
sunk in the lava of your face, you who
I always trusted, who, of all these,
I most believed in, for you were the one,
when I came upon that too-still body of torn
wool while trespassing on that ranch in California,
who told me, before the smell hit, what
had happened simply by your being there,
and now you are full of that wool and I am
become you, attendant, hovering, and there
is no one here for me to tell it to.

I am alone in the Natural History Museum
of Big Basin State Park, standing before you
but not *for* you, a pane having come between us,
writing as if feeding on you, as if your deaths
could sustain me, and it is suddenly clear
to me that you stand, stuffed, for the living
world and I stand, blooded, for the dead.

—AUSTIN SMITH

THE FIELD

Coffee stretches the day out like a buzzing field,
where sun touches everything with its too-bright
fingers, handling common weeds, turning them
almost holy. Heat ushers me past a minute chorus

before I realize what all the insect activity means:
the long, still grass hides some decaying thing
except for its thin odor. And when I exit the field,
lumbering back into the wood's cool shadow,

the expired animal's smell follows for a while.
Beneath the forest's dim lattice, I do not want
shade to relieve my sunburned scalp. I want you
to understand this as simile, to know the field,

pungent and sun-touched, is both more and less
than a field. I want you to know I am the animal
and the insect who feeds on her. He who walks
through the field is somebody else. I am the fur

collapsing into once-firm sinew and the forelegs
washed before touching an unclean body. I am
watching another man pass into the easy dark,
trying to understand why he does not turn back.

I am the udder, which nursed a trembling calf,
the mandible and the larval brood. I am sitting
at the breakfast table, drinking coffee, thinking
about a field, which is the life I want to live.

—DAVID WINTER

ICA(SAU)RUS

When my great grandfather was lying in his casket
the priest compared his body to an old suitcase, one

left behind with superfluous possessions as his soul
flew away to its private, important eternity. On NPR

scientists convene, conspiring plans for interstellar
space travel, since our planet's pretty much cooked,

and is obviously developing fevers to shake us off.
In the Natural History Museum in NY, all of a sudden

they're really big on evolution. Taxidermied seagulls
hang above, soar—us below, soles to marble, eye-level

with terrible lizard remains. On the big wall, the family
tree reminds us birds are alive today, the avian branch

transcending T-Rex, its arrow ascending to promise
of tomorrow after tomorrow—to who knows. Forever.

But once dinosaurs were here. They had heavy bodies—
bones that turned to stone when they flew away.

—Jade Sylvan

THE CURSE

When I arrive, fish rise
belly-up to the mouths of their tanks.
Sewer rats gather at my feet, keel
to their sides, stoic as stones.
Waterlogged snakes float to the brim
of my rose oil tub, eyes gorged, bloated. Bulging.
Sparrows drop from trees in my wake, spattering red.
Above me, squirrels hang
slack-necked from telephone wires.
Glass-eyed elk sprout from the walls
of each restaurant I enter.
At night, owls launch themselves
against my bedroom window, a lonely smudge.
All the neighborhood dogs turn up blue and foaming.
When an elephant rages head-on
through my living room wall,
I cradle her gashed and throbbing trunk,
sop her hemorrhaging eyes, kiss
every seeping wound. I nestle my head
in her gaping bloodmouth and begin to sing.
I sing and sing. I sing hymns to her moaning.
Lullabies and love songs. Nursery rhymes.
I sing and keep singing.
I sing through the morning into dusk.
I sing until the sky goes dark as mud.
I sing until the moon crawls under the sun.
I sing until my voice shatters.

—JEANANNE VERLEE

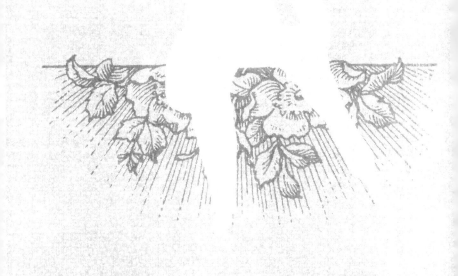

CONTRIBUTORS

NIC ALEA is a Bay Area based writer, and co-host and co-founder of the New Sh!t Show, a reading series focused on the production of new work. Nic's poems have been published or are forthcoming in *Word Riot, Tandem, Rattle*, and *Muzzle Magazine.* Nic is a Lambda Literary Fellow, a semi finalist in Button Poetry's chapbook competition for Sad Boy Slumber Party, and was voted by SF Weekly as one of San Francisco's Best Writers Without a Book Find more at POETRYNICALEA.WORDPRESS.COM.

KAZIM ALI is the author of five collections of poetry, three novels, and three books of nonfiction.

FATIMAH ASGHAR is a nationally touring poet, performer, educator, and writer. Her work has appeared in many journals including *POETRY Magazine, Gulf Coast, BuzzFeed Reader, The Margins, The Offing, Academy of American Poets*, and many others. Her work has been featured on new outlets like PBS, *Teen Vogue, Huffington Post*, and others. In 2011 she created Bosnia and Herzegovina's first Spoken Word Poetry group, REFLEKS while on a Fulbright studying theater in post-genocidal countries. She is a member of the Dark Noise Collective and a Kundiman Fellow. Her chapbook *After* came out on Yes Yes Books fall 2015. She is the writer of *Brown Girls*, a web series that highlights friendships between women of color. Currently she is an MFA candidate at the Helen Zell Writers' Program at the University of Michigan.

CAM AWKWARD-RICH is the author of *Sympathetic Little Monster* (Ricochet Editions, 2016) and the chapbook *Transit* (Button Poetry, 2015). A Cave Canem fellow and poetry editor for *Muzzle Magazine*, his poetry has appeared in *Narrative, The Baffler, Indiana Review* and elsewhere. Currently, Cam is a doctoral candidate in the Program in Modern Thought and Literature at Stanford University and has essays forthcoming/in *Science Fiction Studies* and *Signs: Journal of Women in Culture and Society.*

CORRINA BAIN is a gender-liminal writer-performer. He lives in Brooklyn, New York and works in emergency psychiatry. His poems have been nominated for the Pushcart Prize twice, and have appeared in *Rattle, PANK, A Face to Meet the Faces: An Anthology of Contemporary Persona Poetry, the Everyman's Library book Villanelles,* and elsewhere. See more at CORRINABAIN.COM.

MARY JOY BANG Teachs at Washington University in St. Louis, Missouri. She is the author of six books of poems, including *The Bride of E, Louise in Love,* and *Elegy,* which received the National Book Critics Circle Award. Her translation of Dante's *Inferno,* with illustrations by Henrik Drescher, was published by Graywolf Press in 2012. Her most recent collection, *The Last Two Seconds,* was published by Graywolf in March 2015.

AZIZA BARNES is 21, blk, and alive. Born in Los Angeles, California, she currently lives in Bedstuy, New York. Her first chapbook, *me Aunt Jemima and the nailgun,* was published July 2013 from Button Poetry Press. You can find her work in *Muzzle Magazine, NYU's The Grey Area, West 10th Literary Journal, PLUCK!,* and **Callaloo.** She is a poetry editor at *Kinfolks Quarterly* and a sucker for anything related to Motown.

SCOTT BEAL's poems have recently appeared in *Rattle, Prairie Schooner, Muzzle, Beloit Poetry Journal,* and other journals. He won a Pushcart Prize in 2014. His first book of poems, *Wait 'Til You Have Real Problems,* was published by Dzanc Books in Fall 2014. He serves as writer-in-the-schools for Dzanc Books in Ann Arbor and teaches in the Sweetland Center for Writing at the University of Michigan.

OLIVER BENDORF is a writer and visual artist who grew up in Iowa. His first book of poems, *The Spectral Wilderness,* was selected by Mark Doty for the 2013 Wick Poetry Prize and is forthcoming. His work has been published in *Alaska Quarterly Review, Best New Poets, The Rumpus, Troubling the Line: Trans and Genderqueer Poetry and Poetics,* and elsewhere. He currently lives and teaches in Wisconsin.

LAUREN BERRY received a BA in creative writing from Florida State University and an MFA from the University of Houston, where she won the Inprint Verlaine Prize and served as poetry editor for *Gulf Coast.* From 2009 to 2010 she held the Diane Middlebrook Poetry Fellowship at the Wisconsin Institute. Her first collection of poems, *The Lifting Dress,* was selected by Terrance Hayes to win the National Poetry Series and was released by Penguin in 2011. Lauren currently lives in Houston, Texas where she teaches AP English Language for YES Prep Public Schools, a charter school whose mission is to transform the low-income communities of Houston through college-preparatory education and community service.

TARA BETTS is the author of *Arc & Hue* and the libretto *THE GREATEST!: A Tribute to Muhammad Ali*. Tara is a PhD candidate in English/Creative Writing at SUNY Binghamton University. In addition to her poetry appearing in several anthologies and journals, her scholarly writing has appeared in *The Black Scholar, Obsidian, Xavier Review*, and *Sounding Out!*, a journal in sound studies. Tara has represented Chicago twice at the National Poetry Slam and appeared on HBO's Def Poetry Jam and Jessica Care Moore's SPOKEN. She has worked with young writers in Chicago, New York City, and London. Learn more at WWW.TARABETTS.NET.

MARK BIBBINS is the author of *Sky Lounge*, which received a Lambda Literary Award, *The Dance of No Hard Feelings*, and *They Don't Kill You Because They're Hungry, They Kill You Because They're Full*. He teaches in the graduate writing programs at The New School and Columbia University.

MALACHI BLACK is the author of *Storm Toward Morning* (Copper Canyon Press, 2014). His poems appear widely in journals and anthologies, and his work has several times been set to music and has been featured in exhibitions both in the U.S. and abroad. Malachi is Assistant Professor of English and Creative Writing at the University of San Diego.

SARA BRICKMAN is an author, performer, and activist from Ann Arbor, Michigan. An Artist Trust EDGE fellow, Sara's work has been published or is forthcoming in *Bestiary Magazine, Hoarse, The New*, and *Courage: Daring Poems for Gutsy Girls*. A teacher with Writers in the Schools, Sara is the winner of the third annual Split This Rock Abortion Rights poetry contest, and the 2013 Rain City Women of the World Slam Champion. She has performed her work at venues across North America, including the Bumbershoot Music Festival, Northwest Folklife, and TEDxSeattle. In 2010 she founded a multimedia reading series in her living room called The Hootenanny, to showcase groundbreaking writers and performers. Sara lives and writes in Seattle, Washington, where she would love to do the robot with you.

TRACI BRIMHALL is the author of *Our Lady of the Ruins* (W.W. Norton), winner of the Barnard Women Poets Prize, and *Rookery* (Southern Illinois University Press), winner of the Crab Orchard Series First Book Award. Her poems have appeared in *The New Yorker, Slate, Poetry, The Believer, The New Republic*, and *The Best American Poetry*. She's received fellowships from the Wisconsin Institute for Creative Writing and the National Endowment for the Arts and is an Assistant Professor of Creative Writing at Kansas State University.

EMILY BROWN is a poet from Alabama. Her work is interested in liminal spaces and modes of authenticity. She is interested in hockey and attended the Iowa Writers' Workshop as an MFA student.

JERICHO BROWN has published poems in *The Nation*, *The New Yorker*, *The New Republic*, and *The Best American Poetry*. His first book, *PLEASE*, won the American Book Award, and his second book, *THE NEW TESTAMENT*, was recently released by Copper Canyon Press.

BRENT CALDERWOOD is author of *The God of Longing* (Sibling Rivalry Press, 2014) and Literary Editor for *A&U Magazine*. His poems have appeared in journals and anthologies including *American Poetry Journal*, *Crab Creek Review*, *The Gay & Lesbian Review Worldwide*, and *The Southern Poetry Anthology*. His essays have appeared in the *Chicago Sun-Times*, *OUT Magazine*, the *San Francisco Examiner*, and *Gathered Light: The Poetry of Joni Mitchell's Songs*. Learn more at WWW.BRENTCALDERWOOD.COM.

CHEN CHEN is a University Fellow in poetry at Syracuse University, where he also serves as Poetry Editor for *Salt Hill*. His work has appeared/is forthcoming in *Connotation Press*, *PANK*, *Ghost Proposal*, *Foothill*, *Fjords*, *CURA: A Literary Magazine of Art & Action*, *Nepantla: A Journal for Queer Poets of Color*, among other publications. He has received fellowships from Kundiman, Tent: Creative Writing, and the Saltonstall Foundation.

FRANNY CHOI is the author of *Floating, Brilliant, Gone* (Write Bloody, 2014). She has been a finalist for the Ruth Lilly Poetry Fellowship and multiple national poetry slams. Her poems have appeared in journals such as *Poetry* Magazine and *PANK*, and her work has been featured by the *Huffington Post*, *Feministing*, and *Angry Asian Man*. She is a VONA Fellow, a Project VOICE teaching artist, and a member of the Dark Noise Collective. Franny lives in Providence, Rhode Island.

DOMINIQUE CHRISTINA is an award-winning performance poet and author. She is a National Poetry Slam Champion and two-time Women of the World Poetry Slam Champion. *Heart & Soul* Magazine, *HYSTERIA*, *The Independent*, *Alight*, and various other literary magazines have published her work. Her book *The Bones, The Breaking, The Balm: A Colored Girl's Hymnal* is available from Penmanship Books. She performs and lectures at colleges and universities all over the country. Her work has been featured on *Upworthy* and *Huffington Post*. Dominique is mother to four wildly expressive children who do not use inside voices, ever.

CACONRAD is the author of seven books including *ECODEVIANCE: (Soma)tics for the Future Wilderness* (Wave Books, 2014), *A BEAUTIFUL MARSUPIAL AFTERNOON* (Wave Books, 2012), and *The Book of Frank* (Wave Books, 2010). A 2014 Lannan Fellow, a 2013 MacDowell Fellow, and a 2011 Pew Fellow, he also conducts workshops on (Soma)tic poetry and Ecopoetics. Visit him online at CACONRAD.BLOGSPOT.COM.

EDUARDO C. CORRAL is a CantoMundo fellow. He holds degrees from Arizona State University and the Iowa Writer's Workshop. His poems have appeared in *The Best American Poetry 2012, Beloit Poetry Journal, Jubilat, New England Review, Ploughshares, Poetry, Poetry Northwest, and Quarterly West.* His work has been honored with a "Discovery"/The Nation Award, the J. Howard and Barbara M.J. Wood Prize from Poetry, and writing residencies to the MacDowell Colony and Yaddo. He has served as the Olive B. O'Connor Fellow in Creative Writing at Colgate University and as the Philip Roth Resident in Creative Writing at Bucknell University. *Slow Lightning,* his first book of poems, was selected by Carl Philips as the 2011 winner of the Yale Series of Younger Poets competition. The recipient of a Whiting Writers' Award and a National Endowment for the Arts Fellowship, he currently lives in New York City and spent Spring 2013 teaching at Columbia University.

MEG DAY, recently selected for *Best New Poets of 2013*, is a 2013 recipient of an NEA Fellowship in Poetry and the author of *Last Psalm at Sea Level,* winner of the Barrow Street Press Poetry Prize (2014), *When All You Have Is a Hammer* (winner of the 2012 Gertrude Press Chapbook Contest), and *We Can't Read This* (winner of the 2013 Gazing Grain Chapbook Contest). A 2012 AWP Intro Journals Award Winner, she has also received awards and fellowships from the Lambda Literary Foundation, Hedgebrook, Squaw Valley Writers, and the International Queer Arts Festival. Meg is a PhD fellow in Poetry & Disability Poetics at the University of Utah. Find out more at www. MEGDAY.COM

JOEY DE JESUS is originally from the Soundview neighborhood of the Bronx. He received his BA from Oberlin College and his MFA in Poetry from Sarah Lawrence College. His recent work has appeared or is forthcoming in *The Cortland Review, Beloit Poetry Journal, Devil's Lake, Guernica, Rhino, Versal,* and elsewhere. He has recently become the poetry editor at *Apogee Journal.* He lives in Harlem, New York.

JACOB DODSON wrote crappy poetry in high school. Fortunately, he's no longer in high school anymore. Some of his poetry is still crappy though.

KEITH EKISS is a Jones Lecturer in Creative Writing at Stanford University and a former Wallace Stegner Fellow. He is the author of *Pima Road Notebook* (New Issues Poetry & Prose, 2010) and translator of *The Fire's Journey* (Tavern Books, 2013) by the Costa Rican poet Eunice Odio.

ROBIN EKISS is the author of *The Mansion of Happiness*, which won the 2010 Shenandoah/Glasgow Prize. A former Stegner Fellow and recipient of a Rona Jaffe Award for emerging women writers, Robin's poems have appeared in *The Atlantic Monthly, APR, POETRY, Ploughshares,* and elsewhere. She's on the Advisory Board of *Litquake*, is a contributing editor to *ZYZZYVA* and *Copper Nickel,* and lives in San Francisco, California.

JAMES ELLENBERGER's chapbook, *The Needlework of Their Theft*, was a finalist in the 2014 Iron Horse Literary Review Single Author Competition. His poetry has appeared or is forthcoming in *Sou'Wester, Passages North, THRUSH,* and *Apalachee Review*. After receiving an MFA in creative writing from The Ohio State University in 2012, he worked as a cobbler at Enchanted Shoe Repair. He lives in Cincinnati, Ohio and is pursuing a PhD at the University of Cincinnati.

LAURA EVE ENGEL's work has recently appeared or is forthcoming in *Black Warrior Review, Boston Review, Colorado Review, Columbia Poetry Review, Crazyhorse, Tin House, VOLT*, and elsewhere. A recipient of fellowships from the Wisconsin Institute for Creative Writing and the Provincetown Fine Arts Work Center, she is the Residential Program Director of the University of Virginia Young Writers Workshop.

SHIRA ERLICHMAN is a nationally acclaimed poet, musician, and artist. A Pushcart Prize nominee who has toured the country with some of the nation's leading performers and writers, her prolific and unique style has brought her acclaim as "one of the most original and compelling voices in performance poetry." Her poetry has been featured in NARAL's National ProChoice campaign Free.Will.Power, as well as set to motion by the dancers of the Sound Dance Company. Her award-winning music has appeared in multiple independent films, and on NPR and national TV. She has shared stages with TuNeYaRds, Coco Rosie, and Mirah. Born in Haifa Israel, raised in Brookline, Massachusetts, she now lives in Brooklyn, New York in an indoor treehouse and continues to perform and teach throughout the country.

MARTÍN ESPADA was born in Brooklyn, New York in 1957. He has published almost twenty books as a poet, editor, essayist, and translator. His latest collection of poems from Norton is called *Vivas to Those Who Have Failed*

(2016). Other books of poems include *The Trouble Ball* (2011), *The Republic of Poetry* (2006), *Alabanza* (2003), *A Mayan Astronomer in Hell's Kitchen* (2000), *Imagine the Angels of Bread* (1996), *City of Coughing and Dead Radiators* (1993) and *Rebellion is the Circle of a Lover's Hands* (1990). His many honors include the Shelley Memorial Award, the Robert Creeley Award, the National Hispanic Cultural Center Literary Award, an American Book Award, the PEN/Revson Fellowship and a Guggenheim Fellowship.

TARFIA FAIZULLAH is the author of *Seam* (SIU, 2014), winner of the Crab Orchard Series in Poetry First Book Award. Her poems appear in *American Poetry Review, Ploughshares, New England Review*, and elsewhere. Honors include fellowships and scholarships from Kundiman, the Fulbright Foundation, Bread Loaf, Sewanee, Kenyon Review Writers Workshop, and Vermont Studio Center. She is the Nicholas Delbanco Visiting Professor in Poetry at the University of Michigan Helen Zell Writers' Program.

DINAH FAY is a poet, copywriter, and librettist living in Brooklyn, New York. She co-hosts the Brick City Speaks reading series in Newark, New Jersey, where she is pursuing an MFA in writing from Rutgers University.

ARICKA FOREMAN is a Poetry MFA candidate at Cornell University. A Cave Canem fellow, her work has appeared in *The Drunken Boat, Torch Poetry: A Journal for African American Women, Minnesota Review, Union Station Magazine, Bestiary Magazine*, and *Vinyl Poetry*. She is a Poetry Editor of *MUZZLE Magazine*, and Assistant Editor of *EPOCH*. Aricka is originally from Detroit, Michigan.

CARRIE FOUNTAIN's poems have appeared in *The American Poetry Review, Poetry*, and *Tin House*. Her first collection, *Burn Lake*, was a winner of the 2009 National Poetry Series Award and was published by Penguin in 2010. Penguin will publish her second collection, *Instant Winner*, in 2014. Fountain is writer-in-residence at St. Edward's University in Austin, Texas, where she lives with her husband, the playwright Kirk Lynn, and their children.

MEG FREITAG was born in Maine and raised all over. She now lives in Austin, Texas with a cat named Cheesecake, and a mischievous little black dog named Ramona.

DAPHNE GOTTLIEB is the author and editor of nine books, most recently the poetry book *15 Ways to Stay Alive* as well as co-editor (with Lisa Kester) of *Dear Dawn: Aileen Wuornos in her Own Words.?* She is the editor of *Fucking Daphne: Mostly True Stories and Fictions* and *Homewrecker: An Adultery Reader*, as well as the author of the poetry books *Kissing Dead Girls, Final Girl, Why Things Burn* and *Pelt,* and as the graphic novel *Jokes and the Unconscious* with artist Diane DiMassa. *Final Girl* was the winner of the Audre Lorde Award in Poetry for 2003 from Publishing Triangle.

ERICH HAYGUN has represented Boston, Massachusetts, Providence, Rhode Island, and Vancouver, British Columbia at various poetry slam competitions, and has performed at clubs, theaters, and abandoned zoo cages throughout North America and Europe. Haygun is also a resident, organizer, and recording artist for the DIY record label/ house venue/ social anarchy The Whitehaus Family Record, as well as a community outreach speaker and poet laureate for the Boston Area Rape Crisis Center, and producer of the monthly omni-genre variety show CHEAP SEATS.

REBECCA GAYLE HOWELL is the author of *Render /An Apocalypse* (CSU, 2013), which was selected by Nick Flynn for the Cleveland State University First Book Prize and was a 2014 finalist for *ForeWord Review's* Book of the Year. She is also the translator of Amal al-Jubouri's *Hagar Before the Occupation/ Hagar After the Occupation* (Alice James Books, 2011). Among her awards are two fellowships from the Fine Arts Work Center and a Pushcart Prize. Native to Kentucky, Howell is the Poetry Editor at *Oxford American.*

TONYA INGRAM is the 2011 New York Knicks Poetry Slam champion, a member and co-founder of NYU's poetry slam team, a member of the 2011 Urban Word-NYC team and the 2013 Nuyorican Grand Slam team. She is the author of *Growl and Snare.* Her work has traveled to Ghana, California, Michigan, Texas, Georgia, Massachusetts, Washington D.C., New York, *The Literary Bohemian, Cultural Weekly, Upworthy*, YouTube and season four of *Lexus Verses and Flow.* She is a New York University alumna, a Cincinnati native, a Bronx-bred introvert, and a hopeful Los Angeles folk-child, where she pursues an MFA in Public Practice at Otis College of Art & Design.

NOELLE KOCOT is the author of six books of poetry, including *Poem for the End of Time and Other Poems* (Wave Books, 2006) and *Soul in Space* (Wave, 2013). She's also translated poems of Tristan Corbiere, and they appear in her book, *Poem by Default* (Wave, 2011). She's received numerous awards for her work, including those from The National Endowment for the Arts, The Fund for Poetry, The Academy of American Poets, The Lannan Literary Foundation, and *The American Poetry Review.* Her work is widely anthologized, including in *Postmodern American Poems: A Norton Anthology and Best American Poetry* (2001, 2012, and 2013). She was born and raised in Brooklyn, New York and now lives in the wilds of New Jersey and teaches writing in New York City.

JOSEPH O. LEGASPI is the author of *Imago* (CavanKerry Press), *Subways* (Thrush Press), and two chapbooks: Aviary, Bestiary (Organic Weapon Arts), and winner of the David Blair Memorial Prize. Recent works appeared in *Poets.org, jubilat, The Journal, Painted Bride Quarterly, BLOOM*, and the anthology *Coming Close* (Prairie Lights/University of Iowa Press). He co-founded Kundiman (WWW.KUNDIMAN.ORG), a nonprofit organization serving Asian American literature.

AIREA D. MATTHEWS's first collection of poems, *Simulacra*, received the 2016 Yale Series of Younger Poets Award (Yale University Press, 2017). Her work has appeared in *Best American Poets 2015, American Poets, Four Way Review, The Indiana Review, Michigan Quarterly Review*, and elsewhere. She received the 2016 Rona Jaffe Foundation Writers' Award and was awarded the Louis Untermeyer Scholarship in Poetry from the 2016 Bread Loaf Writers' Conference. She received her B.A. in Economics from the University of Pennsylvania, her M.P.A. from the University of Michigan Ford School of Public Policy, and her M.F.A. from the University of Michigan Helen Zell Writers' Program. Ms. Matthews is working on her second poetry collection, *under/class*, which explores the behavioral and cultural ramifications of poverty.

JAMAAL MAY is the author of *Hum* (Alice James Books), which received the American Library Association's Notable Book Award, Foreword Review's Book of the Year Silver Medal, and an NAACP Image Award nomination. In 2014 Jamaal received over a dozen awards and honors including the Spirit of Detroit Award, a Pushcart Prize, and a Civitella Ranieri Fellowship in Italy. Poems appear widely in magazines and anthologies like *NYTimes.com, Poetry, The New Republic, Ploughshares, Please Excuse this Poem: 100 Poems for the Next Generation* (Penguin), and *The Best American Poetry 2014* (Scribner). Jamaal is a Kenyon Review Fellow and co-directs Organic Weapon Arts with Tarfia Faizullah.

MICHAEL MCGRIFF's latest book is *Our Secret Life in the Movies*, a collection of short stories co-authored with J. M. Tyree. His work has appeared in *The New York Times, The Believer, Tin House*, and on NPR's Weekend Edition.

RACHEL MCKIBBENS is a New York Foundation for the Arts poetry fellow and author of the critically acclaimed volume of poetry, *Pink Elephant* (Cypher Books, 2009.) Regarded as one of the most dynamic speakers in the country, Mckibbens is a legend within the poetry slam community. Her poems, short stories, essays, and creative non-fiction have been featured in numerous journals including *The Los Angeles Review, The Best American Poetry Blog*, and *The Rumpus*.

DEBORAH A. MIRANDA is an enrolled member of the Ohlone Costanoan Esselen Nation of California, and is also of Chumash and Jewish ancestry. The author of two poetry collections—*Indian Cartography*, which won the Diane Decorah Award for First Book from the Native Writer's Circle of the Americas, and *The Zen of La Llorona*, nominated for the Lambda Literary Award—she also has a collection of essays, *The Hidden Stories of Isabel Meadows and Other California Indian Lacunae*, from the University of Nebraska Press. Miranda is an associate professor of English at Washington and Lee University and says reading lists for her students include as many books by "bad Indians" as possible.

MICHAEL MLEKODAY is the author of *The Dead Eat Everything* (Kent State University Press 2014) and a National Poetry Slam Champion. Recent poems appear in *Ploughshares*, *Verse Daily*, *Iron Horse Literary Review*, *PANK*, and other journals.

WILLIAM MORAN was a proud member of the 2011-2013 Austin Poetry Slam national teams, as well as the 2012 and 2013 Austin Poetry Slam Champion and 2013 Southern Fried Haiku Champion. He has co-directed the Texas Grand Slam two years running, featured at venues and taught workshops nationwide, conducted long-term poetry programs at a local juvenile justice center, and released four books and a CD. He is currently the president of Mic Check, a nonprofit poetry and spoken word organization based in Brazos County, Texas. He loves it with all his heart. Also, he is convinced he has the Gulf inside him. He appreciates your concern and well-wishes, but swears he is OK. Really.

TOMÁS Q. MORÍN's poetry collection *A Larger Country* was the winner of the APR/Honickman Prize and runner-up for the PEN/Joyce Osterweil Award. He is co-editor with Mari L'Esperance of the anthology, *Coming Close: 40 Essays on Philip Levine*, and translator of *The Heights of Macchu Picchu* by Pablo Neruda. His poems have appeared in *Slate*, *Threepenny Review*, *Boulevard*, *Poetry*, *New England Review, and Narrative*

SEAN PATRICK MULROY is a 2013 Lambda Literary Fellow, and his work has been published or is forthcoming in *The Bakery, Muzzle, Nailed, The Good Men Project, Assaracus, Rua de Baixo, Network Awesome, Moonshot, Side B, Union Station, Tandem, Frigg, Neon, qu.ee/r, Best Indie Literature of New England, Flicker and Spark: A Contemporary Queer Anthology*, and *Ganymede*. He resides in Boston, Massachusetts while working on multiple projects in music, literature, and television media. He currently co-hosts the Boston Poetry Slam at the Cantab Lounge, and co-curates a monthly LGBTQ reading series, Moonlighting.

HIEU MINH NGUYEN is the author of *This Way to the Sugar* (Write Bloody Press, 2014). His work has also appeared or is forthcoming in publications such as *The Journal, PANK, Anti, Muzzle, decomP, Indiana Review,* and other journals. Hieu is a Kundiman fellow, a recipient of the VERVE grand from Intermedia Arts, and a recipient of the Minnesota Emerging Writer's Grand from The Loft Literary Center.

NAOMI SHIHAB NYE's cats have included Fluffy, Puff, D.C., Jesse, Blackstrap, Jukebox, Hamilton, Scout, Bucky McCloud, and currently, Soxy Durango, the foot-biting raccoon-tailed wonderboy.

LISA OLSTEIN is the author of *Radio Crackling, Radio Gone* (Copper Canyon Press, 2006 and winner of the Hayden Carruth Award), *Lost Alphabet* (Copper Canyon Press, 2009), a *Library Journal* best book of the year, and *Little Stranger* (Copper Canyon Press, 2013), a Lannan Literary Selection. She is a member of the poetry faculty at the University of Texas at Austin.

LADAN OSMAN has received fellowships from the Fine Arts Work Center, Cave Canem, and the Michener Center for Writers. Her work has appeared in *Narrative Magazine, Prairie Schooner, RHINO,* and *Vinyl Poetry.* Her chapbook, *Ordinary Heaven,* appears in *Seven New Generation African Poets* (Slapering Hol Press, 2014). Winner of the Sillerman First Book Prize, *Kitchen-Dweller's Testimony* was published by University of Nebraska Press and Amalion Press. She teaches in Chicago, Illinois.

BLAKE LEE PATE is the editor of *Smoking Glue Gun* and an MFA candidate in the New Writer's Project at the University of Texas, Austin. She is also the Marketing Director for *Bat City Review.* Her poems can be found or are forthcoming in *H_NGM_N, Forklift Ohio, Black Warrior Review, New Delta Review, elimae, Similar:Peaks::.,* and elsewhere.

D.A. POWELL is the author of the trilogy of books *Tea* (Wesleyan, 1998), *Lunch* (2000), and *Cocktails* (Graywolf, 2004)—which was nominated for the National Book Critics Circle Award. His poetry collection *Chronic* (2009) received the Kingsley Tufts Award. His most recent book is *Useless Landscape, or a Guide for Boys: Poems* (2012) won the National Book Critics Circle Award for poetry.

GRETCHEN PRIMACK is the author of two poetry collections, *Kind* (Post-Traumatic Press 2013) and *Doris' Red Spaces* (Mayapple Press 2014). Her poems have appeared in *The Paris Review, Prairie Schooner, The Massachusetts Review, FIELD, Antioch Review, Ploughshares, Best New Poets,* and other journals.

Primack coordinates Ulster Literacy Association's jail program and works at an indie bookstore in Woodstock, New York. Also an advocate for non-human animals, she co-wrote *The Lucky Ones: My Passionate Fight for Farm Animals* (Penguin Avery 2012) with Jenny Brown. She lives in Hurley, New York with her beloved dogs, cats, and human. Her website is WWW.GRETCHENPRIMACK. COM.

PUBBY is the pseudonym of a loose collection of practicing diarists. We privilege empathy for the random, re-creation, r:evolving, revisiting sensations had before, tumbling.

JEREMY RADIN is a poet and actor living in Los Angeles, California where he has helped many friends move. His work has appeared in (or is forthcoming) in *The Rattling Wall, decomP, The Rufous City Review,* and *Hypothetical.* Once, while helping friends move, he tied a couch around his waist and pulled it through a second-story window. His first book, *Slow Dance with Sasquatch,* is available on Write Bloody Publishing.

APRIL RANGER is a 2008 National Poetry Slam finalist, a three-time member of Boston Cantab's National Poetry Slam team, and recipient of the Nicole Dufresne Playwriting Award. Her poems have appeared in *Muzzle Magazine, apt,* and *Off The Coast.* She directed the premiere of her short play, *Civilized Rituals,* at the 2013 Dorchester Fringe Festival. April grew up in Maine and currently lives in Brooklyn, New York. Find out more at WWW. APRILRANGER.COM.

LAYNE RANSOM shamelessly loves Sting's solo albums. Her chapbook *You Are The Meat* was recently released from *H_NGM_N.* She is the design editor for *Stoked Journal,* an online contributor to Vouched Books, and a new MFA candidate in the New Writers' Project at UT Austin. No one can tell her that *The Soul Cages* is not a good record.

CHRISTIAN REES is an alumnus of Loyola University of Maryland's undergraduate writing program. He was born and raised along the banks of the Delaware River, under dogwoods and birches. Recently, he has been published online in *JMWW* and the *Boston Poetry Magazine.* His poem *The Bone House* was nominated for a Pushcart Prize. He divides his time tending a prison library and chopping wood.

SAM SAX is the author of *Madness* (Penguin, 2017), winner of The National Poetry Series selected by Terrance Hayes. His second book *Bury It* will be out on Wesleyan University Press in 2018. He's received fellowships from the National Endowment for the Arts and Lambda Literary.

AUSTIN SMITH has published four chapbooks, and his first full-length collection, *Almanac,* was chosen by Paul Muldoon for the Princeton Series of Contemporary Poets. Poems of his have appeared or will appear in *The New Yorker, Poetry Magazine, VQR, ZYZZYVA, Pleiades, Cortland Review, Sewanee Review,* and others. He also became a Jones Lecturer in fiction at Stanford University.

DANEZ SMITH is the author of the collection *[insert] Boy* (YesYes Books) and the chapbook *hands on ya knees* (Penmanship Books, 2013). Danez is a 2014 Ruth Lilly & Dorothy Sargent Rosenberg Poetry Fellowship Finalist and the recipient of fellowships from the McKnight Foundation, Cave Canem, VONA, and elsewhere. He is a founding member of the multi-genre, multicultural Dark Noise Collective. His writing has appeared in *Poetry Magazine, Ploughshares, Beloit Poetry Journal,* and elsewhere. In Poetry Slam, he is the 2014 NUPIC Champion, a 2011 IWPS finalist, the reigning two-time Rustbelt Individual Champion and was on 2014 Championship Team Sad Boy Supper Club. Danez writes and lives between Oakland, California and St. Paul, Minnesota.

MARY ALICE STEWART studies writing and psychology at Bennington College. She lives in Maine.

JAZ SUFI is a poet, a Bay Area native, an excavator of the human condition, and delighted to make your acquaintance. She competed on the city of Stockton's Pierced Ear Poets national team in 2012 and 2013, was voted audience's choice both years at inkSlam, and represented San Francisco at the 2013 Women of the World Poetry Slam. She was also a featured poet at the 2011 USF Creative Justice Art Show, and has been published in *The Hurt to Hope Anthology.* Sometimes Jaz is sad in her poems, and that's fine, but sometimes she's not, and that's fine, too.

JADE SYLVAN is the author of *Kissing Oscar Wilde* (Write Bloody 2013), *TEN* (Launch Over 2013), and *The Spark Singer* (Spuyten Duyvil 2009). Jade can most frequently be seen getting up to queer feminist performative no-good in and around Cambridge, Massachusetts.

JEANANNE VERLEE is author of *Racing Hummingbirds* (Write Bloody Publishing), recipient of the Independent Publisher Book Award Silver Medal in Poetry. She has also been awarded the Third Coast Poetry Prize and the Sandy Crimmins National Prize for Poetry. Her work has appeared in *The New York Quarterly, Rattle,* and *failbetter,* among others. Verlee wears polka dots and kisses Rottweilers. She believes in you.

A winner of a 2014 Pushcart Prize, **OCEAN VUONG** has received honors from Kundiman, Poets House, The Civitella Ranieri Foundation (Italy), The Elizabeth George Foundation, and The Academy of American Poets. His poems appear in *Poetry, The Nation, Boston Review, Beloit Poetry Journal, Guernica, TriQuarterly*, and *American Poetry Review*, which awarded him the 2012 Stanley Kunitz Prize for Younger Poets. He lives in Queens, New York. Learn more at WWW.OCEANVUONG.COM.

KARRIE WAARALA's work has appeared in journals such as *Iron Horse Literary Review, PANK, The Collagist, Vinyl*, and *Southern Indiana Review*. She is the poetry editor for *the museum of americana* and holds an MFA from the University of Southern Maine. Karrie is the recipient of the 2012 Poctaligo Poetry Prize, a Best of the Net finalist, and a multiple Pushcart Prize nominee. In addition, she has received critical acclaim for her one-woman show, *LONG GONE: A Poetry Sideshow*, which is based on her collection of circus poems. She really wishes she could tame tigers and swallow swords but maybe not at the same time.

PHILLIP B. WILLIAMS is a Chicago, Illinois native. He is the author of the chapbooks *Bruised Gospels* (Arts in Bloom Inc. 2011), *Burn* (YesYes Books, 2013), and the forthcoming *Thief in the Interior* (Alice James Books, 2016). He is a Cave Canem graduate and received scholarships from Bread Loaf Writers Conference and a 2013 Ruth Lilly Fellowship and is also the poetry editor of the online journal *Vinyl Poetry*.

HANIF WILLIS-ABDURRAQIB is from Columbus, Ohio. He is a Pushcart Prize nominated poet, and the author of *Sons Of Noah*, a chapbook from Tired Hearts Press. His poems have been featured in *Radius, Vinyl, Freezeray, joINT, Borderline*, and other journals that are far too kind. He thinks poems can save the world, but also just really wants to talk to you about music and sports.

DAVID WINTER wrote the poetry chapbook *Safe House* (Thrush Press, 2013). His poems also appear in *Atlanta Review, Union Station, Four Way Review*, and other publications. David is currently an MFA student in Creative Writing at The Ohio State University and an Associate Poetry Editor for *The Journal*. He has taught creative writing in jails, at an LGBT senior center, in the Cooper Union Saturday Program, and at Ohio State. David is also working on a literacy research / oral history project about the writing and lives of black poets in Columbus, Ohio.

DEAN YOUNG's books of poems include *Bender: New and Selected Poems* (Copper Canyon Press, 2012). *Primitive Mentor* (University of Pittsburgh Press, 2008), *Embryoyo* (McSweeney's, 2007), *Ready-Made Bouquet* (University of

Pittsburgh Press, 2005), *Elegy on Toy Piano* (2005), *Strike Anywhere* (University Press of Colorado, 1995), which won the Colorado Poetry Prize, *Beloved Infidel* (Wesleyan, 1992), and *Design with X* (1988). He is also the author of *The Art of Recklessness: Poetry as Assertive Force and Contradiction* (Graywolf Press, 2010), a book of prose about poetry, and was a finalist for the Pulitzer Prize for *Skid* (2002) and a finalist for the Lenore Marshall Prize for *First Course in Turbulence* (1999).

MATTHEW ZAPRUDER is the author of four collections of poetry, most recently *Come On All You Ghosts* (Copper Canyon 2010), a New York Times Notable Book of the Year, and *Sun Bear* (Copper Canyon, 2014), as well as a book of prose, *Why Poetry*, from Ecco Press He is also co-translator from Romanian, along with historian Radu Ioanid, of *Secret Weapon: Selected Late Poems of Eugen Jebeleanu* (Coffee House Press, 2007). His poems, essays, and translations have appeared in many publications, including *Tin House, Paris Review, The New Republic, The New Yorker, Bomb, Slate, Poetry,* and *The Believer.* He received a 2011 Guggenheim Fellowship, a William Carlos Williams Award, a May Sarton Award from the Academy of American Arts and Sciences, and a Lannan Foundation Residency Fellowship in Marfa, Texas. An Assistant Professor in the St. Mary's College of California MFA program and English Department, he is also Editor-at-Large at Wave Books. Matthew lives in Oakland, California.

 ACKNOWLEDGEMENTS

Section epigraphs were taken from:

Audre Lorde, *Zami: A New Spelling of My Name* (The Crossing Press, 1982)

Herman Melville, *Moby Dick* (Bantam Classics, 1981, originally publish 1851)

Jonathan Safron Foer, *Eating Animals* (Back Bay Books, 2010)

Kathryn Bond Stockton, *The Queer Child, or Growing Sideways in the Twentieth Century* (Duke University Press, 2009)

George Orwell, *Animal Farm*, (Harcout Brace & Co., 1946)

Mary Ruefle, *Madness, Wrack, and Honey* (Wave Books, 2012)

Bhanu Kapil, *Humanimal* (Kelsey Street Press, 2009)

Aracelis Girmay, *Kingdom Animalia* (BOA Editions Ltd, 2011)

Cary Wolfe, *What is Posthumanism?* (University of Minnesota Press, 2010)

Versions of the following poems have previously appeared in:

"Mass For Pentecost: Canticle For Birds & Waters" by D.A. Powell in *Useless Landscapes, or A Guide for Boys* (Graywolf Press, 2012)

"Fiat Lux" and "Aubade In Which The Bats Tried To Warn Me" by Traci Brimhall in *Rookery* (Southern Illinois University Press, 2010)

"*from* Landscape With Saguaros" by Keith Ekiss in *Pima Road Notebook* (New Issues Poetry & Prose, 2010)

"When Edith Doesn't Have A Body" by Meg Freitag in *Smoking Glue Gun Magazine* vol. 6

"Per Fumum" by Jamaal Mays in *POETRY*

"HERO(i)N" by Airea D. Matthews in *Muzzle*

"The Year Of Dead Geese" and "South" by Rachel Mckibbens in *Into the Dark & Emptying Field* (Small Doggies Press, 2013)

"Sexton Texts From a Bird Conservancy" by Airea D. Matthews in *American Poet*

"Theory of Motion (3): The Sex Question" by Cam Awkward-Rich in *Transit* (Button Poetry, 2015)

"Pounce" by Mark Bibbins in *Sky Lounge* (Graywolf Press, 2003)

"Rain" by Brent Calderwood in *The Southern Poetry Anthology* and *The God of Longing* (SPR, 2014)

"Eastchester Bay [Ending With An Offering]" by Joey De Jesus in *Nepantla*

"Cheap Shot" by Layne Ransom in *Sixth Finch*

"Fishing" by Sam Sax in *The Journal* and *A Guide to Undressing Your Monsters* (Button Poetry 2014)

"Precipice" by Oliver Bendorf in *The Spectral Wilderness* (Kent State University Press, 2014)

"Cain" by Jericho Brown in *The Rumpus*

"How To Kill A Hog" by Rebecca Gayle Howell in *Render / An Apocalypse* (CSU Press, 2013)

"The Cow" by Michael McGriff in *Home Burial* (Copper Canyon Press, April 2012).

"Annie Mason's Collie" by Franny Choi in *Floating, Brilliant, Gone* (Write Bloody Press, 2014)

"Laika" by Tomás Morin in *Boulevard Magazine* and A Larger Country (Copper Canyon Press 2012)

"Exile The Dragon-Tailed And The Rabbit-Eared Among You" by Lisa Olstein in *Little Stranger* (Copper Canyon, 2013)

"The Dogs And I Walked Our Woods" and "The Workers" by Gretchen Primack in *Kind* (2013)

"Fighters" by April Ranger in *Boston Poetry Slam: 20 Years At The Cantab Lounge* (Crooked Treehouse Press, 2013)

"The Ghost Of The Author's Mother Has A Conversation With His Fiancée About Highways." by Hanif Willis-Abdurraqib in *(RE)Cap*

"Mosque In Galilee" by Kazim Ali, *Taos Journal*

"Aubade For One Still Uncertain Of Being Born" by Meg Day in *Last Psalm at Sea Level* (Barrow Street Press, 2014)

"Elegy For An Electrocuted Elephant" by Robin Ekiss in *Ninth Letter*

"*from* I Write To You From The Sea" by Laura-Eve Engel in *The Denver Quarterly*

"Moose" by Joseph Legaspi in *Aviary, Beastiary* (Organic Weapons Arts, 2014)

"Deer" by Deborah A. Miranda in *Indian Cartography* (Greenfield Review Press, 1999)

"Tanning Process" by Christian Rees in *Boston Poetry Magazine*

"Juxtaposing The Road Kill With My Body" by Danez Smith in *Indiana Review*

"Eurydice" by Ocean Vuong in *The Nation* and *NO* (YesYesBooks, 2013)

"The Earthquake She Slept Through" by Mary Jo Bang in *Academy of American Poet's Poem-A-Day* and forthcoming in *The Last Two Seconds* (Graywolf Press, 2015)

"Metamorphosis" by Malachi Black in *Storm Toward Morning* (Copper Canyon Press, 2014)

"Aubade Ending With The Death Of A Mosquito" by Tarfia Faizullah in *Blackbird* and *Seam* (Southern Illinois University Press, 2014)

"Ode To The White-Line-Swallowing Horizon" by Jamaal May in *Pen America*

"Domestic Buildup" by Blake Lee Pate in *H_NGM_N sixteen*

"Black Witch Moth" by Philip B. Williams in *Nashville Review*

"Want" by Eduardo Corral in *Slow Lightening* (Yale University Press, 2012)

"Ode To My Cat Euclid" by Noelle Kocot in *Poem for the End of Time and Other Poems* (Wave Books, 2006)

"Self Portrait, Wearing Bear Skull As Mask" by Michael Mlekoday in *Ninth Letter* and *The Dead Eat Everything* (Kent State University Press, 2014)

"Haunted" by Naomi Shihab Nye in *TRANSFER* (BOA Editions Ltd, 2011)

"Lady, That's A Lemur Get Out Of My Crotch" by Mary Alice Stewart in *The Silo*

"Idaho" by Matthew Zapruder in *Academy of American Poets Poem a Day*

"After" by Fatimah Asghar in *Gulf Coast*

"How To Make A Shadow" by Ladan Osman in *Narrative* and *Ordinary Heaven* (Slapering Hol, 2014)

"The Field" by David Winter in *Safe House* (Thrush Press, 2013)

by Lauren Gilmore
Outdancing the Universe

by Rob Gray
The Immaculate Collection/The Rhododendron and Camellia Year Book (1966)

by Joseph Edwin Haeger
Learn to Swim

by Lindsey Kugler
HERE.

by Wryly T. McCutchen
My Ugly and Other Love Snarls

by Michael McLaughlin
Countless Cinemas

by Johnny No Bueno
We Were Warriors

by A.M. O'Malley
Expecting Something Else

by Stephen M. Park
High & Dry
The Grass is Greener

by Christine Rice
Swarm Theory

by Michael N. Thompson
A Murder of Crows

by Sarah Xerta
Nothing to Do with Me

CPSIA information can be obtained
at www.ICGtesting.com
Printed in the USA
FFOW02n1408070418
46161341-47342FF